Dear Reader:

The book you are about ~~to~~ ... St. Martin's True Crime Lib ... ~~calls~~ lls "the leader in true crime ... ng account of the latest, mo ... the national attention. St. Ma ... publisher of Tina Dirmann's VANISHED AT SEA, the story of a former child actor who posed as a yacht buyer in order to lure an older couple out to sea, then robbed them and threw them overboard to their deaths. John Glatt's riveting and horrifying SECRETS IN THE CELLAR shines a light on the man who shocked the world when it was revealed that he had kept his daughter locked in his hidden basement for 24 years. In the Edgar-nominated WRITTEN IN BLOOD, Diane Fanning looks at Michael Petersen, a Marine-turned-novelist found guilty of beating his wife to death and pushing her down the stairs of their home—only to reveal another similar death from his past. In the book you now hold, ONE DARK NIGHT, Kevin McMurray examines a sensational case that includes sex, greed, deceit, and murder.

St. Martin's True Crime Library gives you the stories behind the headlines. Our authors take you right to the scene of the crime and into the minds of the most notorious murderers to show you what really makes them tick. St. Martin's True Crime Library paperbacks are better than the most terrifying thriller, because it's all true! The next time you want a crackling good read, make sure it's got the St. Martin's True Crime Library logo on the spine—you'll be up all night!

Charles E. Spicer, Jr.,
Executive Editor, St. Martin's True Crime Library

ST. MARTIN'S PAPERBACKS TRUE CRIME LIBRARY TITLES BY KEVIN F. McMURRAY

One Dark Night
Desire Turned Deadly
A Family Cursed
If You Really Loved Me

ONE DARK NIGHT

KEVIN F. McMURRAY

ONE DARK NIGHT

Copyright © 2010 by Kevin F. McMurray.

All rights reserved.

For information address St. Martin's Press, 175 Fifth Avenue, New York, NY 10010.

EAN: 978-0-312-94414-8

Printed in the United States of America

St. Martin's Paperbacks edition / February 2010

St. Martin's Paperbacks are published by St. Martin's Press, 175 Fifth Avenue, New York, NY 10010.

10   9   8   7   6   5   4   3   2   1

Special thanks to M.H. Rowland for her
superb transcription, research and editing skills.

ONE
DARK
NIGHT

CHAPTER ONE:

911

AS ANYONE WHO has ever lived or spent time in New York City will avow, it is not a city to be loved and cast aside lightly. Its vibrating pulse beats intuitively to the 10 million people who call it home, and the city's spirit silently melds into the psyche of all who pass through its precincts.

Carlos and Peggy Perez-Olivo were no different. New York City was a passion they had always shared. From the days of their courting to their years living in the Bronx, they had become addicted to the Big Apple. Even though they no longer lived in the city, they were at heart New Yorkers, and returned to many of their old haunts in their free time. And free time was something that, until recently, had been in short supply.

For years Carlos had labored long legal hours in New York, although usually not in Manhattan. Most of his business had been conducted in the blue-collar borough of Queens. Queens is in the shadow of the most famous skyline in the world, and, though Carlos' office was just a couple of subway stops from midtown Manhattan, it was still a world away from the glamour and pizzazz of the "city that never sleeps," immortalized in Sinatra's "New York, New York."

But Queens was no more for Carlos. Queens had turned from the lure of an overflowing honey pot to a lurid tale of failure for the Puerto Rican attorney. And although he wished his separation from the outer borough had been more on his terms, he couldn't pretend that he missed the early mornings and late nights of the grinding legal day. In fact, he couldn't withhold a slight smile of relief when he remembered that he no longer had to spend any time there. Ever optimistic, despite such a dramatic lurch into misfortune, Carlos, at 58 years of age, was all for this change in his life's structure and he was sure the future was brighter. He had plans.

For Peggy the city of her dreams was still a world away. Peggy had reluctantly given up this vibrant city and her adopted hometown to relocate to the city's northern suburbs to raise her and Carlos' three children. Chappaqua in Westchester County was not so bad, though. She could be in Manhattan in just 45 minutes by train or even faster if she opted to drive in. But now that her kids were pretty much all grown up, she was no closer to moving back to Manhattan than she'd been when she was pushing baby strollers around in the bucolic tree-lined streets of the village of Chappaqua.

Throughout the transient years of early parenthood, it was her future dreams that had held her on course: dreams that she and Carlos would one day move back to Manhattan— when the kids had moved out most likely. Manhattan had always been the hub of their lives. Apart from her job, there soon wouldn't be anything to keep them anchored in Chappaqua. Maybe when their daughter, 17-year-old Alysia, went off to college, it would be a good time to move. But for now, she and her husband had settled, almost unwittingly, into suburban life.

Peggy knew Carlos would love to live in the city, and was confident she could persuade him to return. This was, after all, the city he'd been conceived in, and gone to college in. He had even spent a year in law school in Manhattan.

For some years, having left full-time work to be a full-time mother, Peggy had felt adrift from other adults, lost amongst the trappings of motherhood and devoid of the stimulation of her earlier career. But now she was settled and established as a teacher's aide in the Chappaqua school system and she had to admit she liked the work and didn't want to leave it. So Carlos and Peggy had to content themselves with driving into town on weekends and spending the day absorbing the culture of Gotham as visitors.

Peggy and Carlos had originally planned a visit for Saturday, November 11, 2006, and had been looking forward to it, but at the last minute they learned that the reason for their trip, the foreign-language film *Volver*, with the Argentine actress Penélope Cruz, had sold out. Disappointed, but resolved to reschedule, they checked their diaries and found they were going to be free the following Saturday—November 18, 2006—and this time Carlos would purchase the tickets in advance over the Internet.

Their enthusiasm having been put on hold for a week, they were now both very much looking forward to the trip into town.

But despite its pale comparison to the exciting city to the south, Chappaqua was getting interesting. Lately it was getting the attention of the media, and for good reason: the Clintons had arrived.

The epitome of a power couple, the Clintons, in 1999, soon to depart the White House, had chosen Chappaqua after a long and much publicized home search in the suburbs around the city. It was an open secret that Hillary was planning a run for a New York seat in the United States Senate that was up for grabs with the impending retirement of much-beloved and respected Daniel Patrick Moynihan.

Chappaqua got the nod. The house the Clintons chose was a bargain at $1.7 million, located on a quiet cul-de-sac near the center of town. Hillary had her official New York residence and soon-to-be-former President of the United States William Jefferson Clinton was now just a short commute from Manhattan, where he planned to establish an office to conduct his post-presidency business.

Wealthy and picture-perfect, and a left-of-center outpost in a Republican county, Chappaqua welcomed the former First Family with open arms. A retired President of the United States living in their midst would only enhance

Chappaqua's image—and in the process drive up real estate values in the 9.4-square-mile community. Having a United States Senator living in town didn't hurt either.

Not that the town was hard-pressed for the wealthy and influential. Actors Alan Arkin and Vanessa Williams, and Kiss lead guitarist Ace Frehley could have formed a welcoming committee to their community.

Chappaqua seems to have it all: an eloquent beauty, a vibrant median age of 39 for residents, an impressive median family income of $180,451 and an average house value of $562,000.

It was a different world from the one the Clintons had known in Little Rock, Arkansas—or, for that matter, Washington, D.C.

Despite having prestigious neighbors, the Perez-Olivo family lived an ordinary life with a regular routine. Like many another middle-aged couple, they were concerned with the health issues of aging. Carlos and Peggy had gotten into the habit of doing a little power-walking. Peggy had been having some problems with sciatica, a troublesome nerve condition that shot a searing pain down her leg from her hip, and the walking seemed to have helped.

With the dawning of November 18, 2006, the day that would change his life forever, Carlos arose at 8:30 AM expecting to power-walk as normal. That day, however, Peggy decided to skip the walk in preparation for their visit, so instead, Carlos drove over to the health club he belonged to and had a workout.

Carlos had always been active in sports. He loved to play pick-up basketball at Club Fit, which was just a few miles from his home in the adjoining community of Briarcliff Manor. Feeling good after his workout, Carlos thoughtfully stopped at the D'Agostino supermarket at 12:30 PM to pick up a frozen pizza for him and his wife to share, to save Peggy having to make lunch, and satisfy their appetifes until dinnertime at a Manhattan restaurant.

By 3:30 PM they were ready at last. As they pulled the door shut, Peggy glanced over at her husband, who, as ever, was casually but smartly dressed. Peggy's glance was smilingly returned by her husband as they climbed into the car and the couple finally left for the city with enough time, Carlos believed, to get to the theater for the 4 PM show. Wistful perhaps in her thoughts of living in Manhattan and thereby avoiding these one-off visits, Peggy didn't know she would never come in to the city again.

The Chelsea Theater was located on 23rd Street just off 9th Avenue, the couple's favorite area of Manhattan. Chelsea, a delightfully quirky neighborhood on the Lower West Side, was host to a plethora of cultural delights. One of them was cuisine. When Carlos and Peggy emerged from the movie theater at approximately 6:20 PM, it was still a little early for dinner. Carlos didn't need to be told that his wife would be happy to kill some time at one of her favorite pastimes: window-shopping.

Chelsea has an eclectic mix of residential apartment buildings, brownstones and rehabilitated warehouses chaotically interspersed with a wide array of shops, ethnic delis and restaurants and art galleries. Peggy especially loved the area because of the appealingly eccentric shops that didn't make it into suburbia.

Chelsea, known also as the floral center of Manhattan, was a delight to walk through, as the air was full of fragrances of every possible species of flower, from dog daisies to orchids. The aromas aroused memories of an earlier existence in this exotic city and again Peggy wished she lived in Manhattan.

With the onset of evening a myriad of shop lights glittered an invitation to buy their wares, and Carlos and Peggy sauntered very slowly, making their way up to 5th Avenue with a vague idea of finding a place to dine and window-shop. A vintage clothing store caught Peggy's fancy. Good-naturedly, Carlos idled outside while his wife explored. After a few minutes his wife beckoned to him. Dutifully he stepped inside. A $60 topaz ring had caught her attention. Wryly,

Carlos pointed out that she already had a similar ring, for which they had paid $25. Accepting her husband's gentle refusal to buy the ring, Peggy was content to leave the store without making a purchase.

Continuing their stroll along 5th Avenue, Peggy stopped in at more shops. Carlos patiently indulged his wife's slow progress. Finally the couple arrived at a restaurant Carlos knew.

Sevilla is a Cuban restaurant Carlos had patronized as far back as his college days at Columbia University. But tonight it was too busy for them, with a long line of people snaking out the door waiting for a table. After checking out another eatery and finding it also too busy, Carlos flagged down a taxicab to take them back to the lot where their car was parked.

They decided to dine at a French restaurant they both knew. Carlos drove the car down to a parking garage near the restaurant, Frere Jacques, located on 37th Street. They got there around 8 PM, and were quickly seated.

They began by ordering the first of a number of Cosmopolitans, their favorite cocktail. Mellow with the way the trip had gone and relaxed with her Cosmopolitan in this most cosmopolitan of cities, as the meal progressed, Peggy carefully brought their idle chitchat around to a more serious discussion. Peggy told her husband he was being overprotective of their teenage daughter Alysia and that he had to give the girl a little more space. The 16-year-old was on the threshold of womanhood, and no longer their "little girl." How many fathers have gulped at this speech and realized the wisdom of the words? Tactfully leaving the subject for due consideration, the conversation moved along to a discussion on the couple's proposed plans for Thanksgiving, just a week away.

Had Carlos realized how many Cosmopolitans he had drunk over the course of the hour and a half in the restaurant (he had had five), maybe he wouldn't have driven, and the day would have ended very differently. Peggy likewise, after three relaxing drinks and a satisfying meal, may have been lulled into an unexpected somnolence—which was to prove fatal.

The couple left the restaurant at around 9:30 PM. In the car, Carlos got a phone call from a friend from his college days, Frank Furillo. Frank was bored and decided to call his friends to see what they were up to. They spoke for a bit and agreed they should meet sometime soon. Peggy got on the phone to say hi and seconded Carlos' desire for them to get together. Peggy then placed a call to their daughter to let her know they were on their way home. They chatted some, with Peggy teasing her a little about her first date with a boy. Peggy told her daughter she loved her before ending the call.

Before reaching the Henry Hudson Bridge, Carlos stopped at a gas station that he knew in the Inwood section of northern Manhattan. There were a lot of cars backed up at the pumps. Glancing at his fuel gauge, he figured he had enough gas to get to them back to Chappaqua, where the gas was cheaper anyway. Carlos, the spendthrift, hated paying exorbitant fuel prices, and routinely drove out of his way just to save a few pennies per gallon. He got back on the parkway and headed for home.

Instead of taking the Saw Mill River Parkway to Chappaqua, Carlos took the Taconic State Parkway. The Taconic was a longer route home, but didn't have traffic lights like the Saw Mill did. There was also an all-night Exxon gas station just off the Taconic in the Millwood section of New Castle, of which the village of Chappaqua was a part. Carlos regularly patronized it, since it had the lowest prices in town.

Some thirty minutes later he exited the parkway at the Route 100/9A exit. Driving north along Route 100, Carlos looked over at his wife and saw that she had fallen asleep.

The road that paralleled the Taconic was dark and quiet. Carlos didn't see another car on the road. They just had a few more miles to go before they reached the Exxon station.

It had been a cool, clear, moonless November evening with the mercury beginning its slow but inevitable downward march when Nile Clarke got the call.

Up until then it had been a fairly quiet evening. Not much action in the northern part of Westchester County and the southern end of Putnam County from a 911 dispatcher's point of view. She had just hung up on a call from a concerned citizen informing authorities about a drunk driver he had seen weaving all over the road on the Taconic Parkway. Clarke picked up the next call before the second ring.

The next twelve and a half minutes were to be the start of what was to become one of the most infamous murder trials of 2008. As these extracts from the call imply, the caller was desperately in need of help. And although the call begins with a degree of calm, it quickly deteriorates into chaos:

> **Carlos:** [gasping and voice rising] That's why I'm taking . . . I'm taking my wife to the . . . [voice hysterical] I'm telling you I'm going to the hospital . . . I think she may be . . . I think . . . [very heavy gasping]
>
> **PO:** Okay . . . where?
>
> **Carlos:** she got shot . . . [cry and voice rising again]
>
> **911 Operator:** Okay, okay.
>
> **Police Officer:** Okay. Take it easy. She got shot, you say?

Despite the constant interruption of the police and the dispatcher, Carlos Perez-Olivo remained focused only on what he believed was the right thing for him to do. He had to get to the hospital at all costs.

> **Carlos:** I can't stop. . . . I can't stop. . . . I've got to get my wife to the hospital. . . . I can't stop. . . . I can't stop. . . . I'm . . . I'm all right. . . . I'll get there. . . . Don't worry. . . . Just . . . just . . . try . . . try and get a patrol car and see if you can get this guy. . . . Please, please, please . . .

Police Officer: Okay. What . . . What . . . What kind of car is it?

And it is only halfway through the call that the police officer realizes that Carlos is himself wounded.

Carlos: I'm in a . . . I'm in a . . . I'm in a Mit . . . in a [breaks off with groans]

Police Officer: Are you injured . . . Are you injured too?

Carlos: Yeah . . . Yeah . . . Shot . . . Yes . . . Yes . . . Yes, I'm shot . . . I'm fine, fine . . . I'm . . . I'm . . . I'm shot on the side . . . and I'm fine. . . .

Police Officer [overtalking, almost inaudible]: Sir, I believe . . .

Carlos: I got shot also, see, I'm going to need some . . . some medical attention. Please put a . . . put a hold now, please . . . [inaudible] You've got to get to the son-of-a-bitch. . . .

Police Officer: Listen to me. Listen to me. [overtalking—inaudible] I've got to take care of you first . . . Both of you . . .

Carlos [loud]: Forget about me . . . My wife . . . My wife is important, not [voice pitch escalating] me. . . . Not me. . . . Not me. . . . Not me. . . . [Voice fading]

Police Officer: Sir, I . . .

Carlos: [high pitched and crying] I'm not pulling over. . . . I'm not pulling over. . . . I'm not pulling over. . . . I'm not . . . I'm not . . . I'm not pulling over. . . . I'm not . . . I'm not pulling over . . . [Gibberish cries, repetition]

The call was to be eventually lost, possibly as Carlos reached the hospital.

For the inhabitants of Chappaqua, it was to be the beginning of a shameful period in the town's history.

CHAPTER TWO:

AMBITION

BORN IN NEW York City on May 1, 1948, Carlos Perez-Olivo was the product of the first wave of Puerto Ricans who flocked to New York City in what was called "the Great Migration" of 1946 where some 40,000 people settled in New York. Since the island was given Commonwealth status in 1917, after being a United States "possession" since the Spanish-American War in 1898, Puerto Ricans had always been free to travel back and forth between the Caribbean island and the US mainland. But it was with the advent of air travel that the numbers traveling—and migrating—to the US swelled in the late 1940s and 1950s. It was a freedom that Carlos would take advantage of over the course of his whole life, starting when he was just three months old.

His mother, who had come north to get her education, had met Carlos' father, a Cuban, in New York. It was a short relationship, of which the only product was Carlos. The young mother returned to Puerto Rico with Carlos, knowing she would need the help of her extended family to rear him. There, Carlos' grandparents took over the responsibility of raising a fatherless child.

After three years in San Juan, the family moved to the remote central part of the island, where Carlos' grandfather was bishop in the Presbyterian church. Carlos' grandfather had eight children, the oldest a son named Ramon, who was married to a woman named Mercedes. The childless couple eagerly assumed the responsibilities of parenting young Carlos. The boy took to them right away and, to this day, he always considers them his "real" mother and father.

Carlos had a wonderful childhood on the island, where, he says, he was "the apple of the family eye." Ramon was an attorney, and Mercedes a teacher who saw to it that Carlos got an early start. By the time he was 4, Carlos could read and write. When he entered primary school he was well grounded in language skills, and being an early maturing boy, he was head and shoulders taller than his classmates. Bored by the lack of challenge—academically and physically—Carlos became a bit of a mischief-maker. Consequently, he was "thrown out" of a number of private schools. His dad eventually enrolled him at the American School, where he polished up his English and blossomed academically.

He would eventually apply to a number of colleges. Columbia University was just one of the many prestigious universities where he was accepted. That it was in New York made the decision to enroll simple for him. Carlos was thrilled to be going back to the city of his birth. Despite the fact that he'd left New York as an infant, he always considered it to be his real home and where he belonged.

Carlos joined no fraternities, no groups active in the volatile campus politics of the sixties. Just one day in the Boy Scouts had given him all he needed to know about participating in groups. It wasn't that he was unsociable, it was that he was no "joiner." Structured environments would always be a problem for him. He says he was not the best student at Columbia, explaining that the hardest thing was getting into the school, the general feeling being "If you were smart enough to get in, you were too smart to flunk out."

An avid basketball player, Carlos didn't go out for the school team, since he had promised his father he would focus on his schoolwork. God knew there were plenty of other distractions in the Big Apple he had to deal with.

Acquiescing to his father's wishes, Carlos, upon graduating with a BA, attended the University of Puerto Rico (UPR) School of Law, his dad's alma mater. Carlos hated it:

"It was very political. The school was heavily populated with those who were fervent proponents of Puerto Rican independence," Carlos said.

Carlos, who had a propensity to speak English to his professors, was ostracized by his fellow students as an "American." If he were a proud Puerto Rican, they believed, he would speak only Spanish and not the language of their imperialist subjugators.

Thanks to a near-photographic memory, Carlos fared well in law school. He was, however, miserable at UPR. Fearing he would come to hate the law, his father finally intervened. He arranged for his adopted son to matriculate for a year at Columbia Law School with the understanding that he would complete his last year back at UPR.

Carlos was overjoyed to be back at Columbia and in New York. He fell back in with his old crowd and, despite a busy social life, managed to do well in school. Obligated, Carlos returned to the Caribbean island and finished his studies knowing that somehow he would make his way back to New York.

His father, fulfilling a dream, brought his son into the practice. He was happier still, as there was a lot of work in federal court that was all heard in English, and his son had a better command of the language than he did. One month after being sworn in as an officer of the court, Carlos found himself in front of the busy federal bench defending a paying client. In the first year of his professional career, instead of clerking or taking the "second chair" for more senior attorneys, Carlos was actually trying cases. He was good too. That year, he didn't lose a case in the nine he tried. His success begat more business, and the precocious Carlos, just 25, found himself to be a hot commodity in the insular world of Puerto Rican jurisprudence. His skills were needed. Puerto Rico was a major transit point in the Colombian drug trade in the mid-1970s. Consequently there were a lot of drug busts, which in turn produced a need for defense attorneys.

Carlos loved it and was, at the time, content to practice in the backwaters of federal criminal law. It was a date with an Eastern Air Lines stewardess by the name of Peggy Hall that changed his priorities.

CHAPTER THREE:

A FUN-LOVING GIRL

BORN ON SEPTEMBER 3, 1951, the healthy baby girl was baptized Peggy Louise Hall a few days later at a neighborhood Catholic church in a comfortable section of Lexington, Kentucky. She joined a growing family of five, with four more children to follow over the years. Her sister Marie (not her real name) is hard-pressed to recall anything abnormal about the upbringing of herself and her seven sisters and one brother. It was what she called "your average middle-class Catholic home."

Peggy's father was a weatherman with the government's National Weather Service stationed in Lexington. Mr. Hall worked different shifts at the station, so he was home at different times during the day, which was unusual for those years. Easy-going and a calm presence in the household, Mr. Hall gave his kids more space then most kids of the day. He also gave his fourth child an unusual name by church standards. In Catholic primary school, Marie remembers, her parents had to go in and complain because one nun kept making Peggy write the name "Margaret" on her papers. "My parents had to take her baptismal certificate to school to stop it," Marie recounted.

Despite what Marie calls a "totally normal family," she added that, "If you talked to my seven brothers and sisters, you would get seven different stories about Peggy's life and our lives and growing up in Lexington." Even to this day she marvels when talking to her sisters and her brother how differently they perceived the same experiences, even though they were a close-knit family.

The Hall family was not particularly well-off, but they weren't in need of anything either. Marie says one of the pluses of a family of nine kids was they had each other, and for the most part found companionship amongst themselves. They didn't feel the need to reach outside the family for friendship and for things to do.

As children, they did all the typical things kids did in those times: tag, roller-skating and ball games. But it was Peggy who chose what games to play. Activities didn't get started until Peggy arrived. Marie recalled that Peggy was the life of the party; she was a rabble-rouser, and she was loved for it.

It was Peggy, her sister reminisced, who taught her to roller-skate and was the one who stood by and held the bike when Marie was learning how to ride the two-wheeler. In a lot of ways, Marie says, Peggy was her mentor. She taught her younger sister as a teen how to fend off "unwanted situations" and how to strike out on her own path.

Peggy was the Hall child who did the trailblazing. When it came time, the Hall kids got to choose what high school they wanted to attend, Lexington Catholic or Tates Creek, the local high school. Peggy opted for Tates. Marie said her older sister (by 18 months) wanted a wider social life than she was likely to get at a conservative Catholic school. It was not all just books and classes to the vibrant, outgoing, well-liked Peggy.

All the girls were required to have chaperones when dating. Marie, however, would often double-date with her big sister, and thereby placate their mom and dad.

But Peggy, says her sister, was itching to get out of Lexington.

"She wanted an exciting life, and settling down in Lexington was not the answer for her. Peggy would ultimately become the only child in the family not to marry a local or stay in Lexington to work.

After graduating from high school in 1969, Peggy worked in town for a year, then applied for and got a position as a stewardess on Eastern Air Lines. Considered at the time to be a plum job that traditionally employed only single and attractive women, Peggy saw it as a ticket out of Lexington.

Marie says it was all very exotic to her, especially since none of the Hall girls had even been on an airplane. Topping it off, Peggy would eventually be based out of New York.

Thanksgiving was a time for the Hall family to reunite. Weddings and other special occasions were also well attended by the tight-knit family. It was during one of her trips home that Peggy confessed to her sister that the stewardess job was not as glamorous as some people thought. What she missed most, she told Marie, was having a home and someone to come home to. It seemed most of her downtime was spent in a small New York apartment with a collection of roommates or by herself in a hotel room. Peggy was very lonely.

But there always was the travel, which Peggy loved. From New York she got to travel all over the country. One of her regular routes was New York to San Juan, Puerto Rico.

CHAPTER FOUR:

LIVING THE DREAM

"I WAS FINALLY making money on my own. I had people coming to see me every weekend, people sent by mutual friends to look me up," Carlos said about his life as a bachelor lawyer in Puerto Rico's capital city.

One of those looking him up was 23-year-old Peggy Hall. They met for dinner together with two other mutual friends who effected the introduction. It was Carlos' and his buddies' tried-and-true strategy of having two others along in case the date was a disaster in the making. As it turned out, Carlos didn't need the cover. He monopolized the pretty girl's time by dancing most of the night away with her. The following day Carlos took her to see the El Yunque rain forest, a popular tourist attraction outside San Juan. By the end of the day, it seemed to Carlos that Peggy was someone he had known all his life.

Within a week, Carlos had notified all his girlfriends that he couldn't see them anymore. Peggy began to spend all her free time with Carlos in San Juan.

Carlos' college buddy Frank Furillo remembers Carlos spending a week with him in Venezuela for a reality check. Frank said Carlos was miserable without Peggy's presence. On his return to San Juan he wasted no time, and proposed to the pretty American girl. Peggy, however, was in no hurry—they had been dating just three months. She wanted to live together before she would make a commitment. Carlos, citing old-fashioned, conservative, church-going parents, insisted on getting married.

She eventually acquiesced, and they tied the knot unofficially before a justice of the peace. Six months later, on February 7, 1976, they had a church wedding in front of the whole family in Lexington.

Carlos was welcomed into the Hall family, where the young Puerto Rican was made to feel like a member. Carlos found them to be fair, open-minded people and a pleasure to be around.

The Lexington wedding was not a big one, but, as Peggy's sister Marie recalls, "a family type of wedding." What was different about it was that the reception was at a restaurant and not in a hall, as were most of the Hall weddings. Seven daughters' weddings to pay for, no doubt, explained that custom. What Marie remembers most about it was Peggy's gorgeous dress and how glamorous she looked. Her sister was so beautiful and blessed, she thought, and as a couple, Peggy and Carlos were very worldly and exciting compared to the rest of the family. They traveled, dined out a lot in fancy restaurants, and even ordered wine by the bottle with their meals. Marie was very proud of her older sister, and grew to love Carlos as well.

Carlos says he never really experienced prejudice, either with his white family-in-law, or in the States. He submits that it may have gone over his head, unrecognized by him, but he believes he has always been treated fairly and never suffered because of his ethnicity. Something his grandfather said to him guided his life: "You're not better than anybody, and nobody is better than you."

As a result, he always frowned on fellow islanders who would claim that prejudice prevented them from succeeding in their endeavors.

Despite a religious background, Carlos never was much of a churchgoer and gravitated toward agnosticism, eventually coming to consider himself an atheist. Carlos couldn't square all the bad there is in the world with an all-healing god of love: "I have a hard time believing that there is a god when bad things happen to good people."

But it was Peggy who prevailed in how their children would be raised. She believed they should be given a religious upbringing, and then, when they were old enough, allowed to make their own decisions. And so it was.

In Puerto Rico, Peggy had a bet with a friend that she would not have a baby within the first year of the marriage. She lost the bet, having gotten pregnant after eleven months, and she gave birth to Carlos Jr., called Carlitos, on October 3, 1977.

At this point, Peggy was itching to get off the island. Carlos said she hated living there, mainly because she couldn't speak Spanish. There also was a tangible antagonism against Americans. At the time, there was not even any English-language TV on the island. It was all very depressing to her. Carlos said it was not the best of times on the island, and even though they lived in a good neighborhood, the possibility of her being a victim of crime always worried him.

Professionally it was also time for Carlos to move on. His father had retired a year and a half earlier, so Carlos felt no obligation to stay. He had also found out that having put in five years before the federal bench in San Juan, he was entitled to reciprocity between the US Commonwealth of Puerto Rico and New York, and could practice law in the state. It was time to return to his real home.

He was offered a job at a large law firm for a substantial salary, but the prospect of pursuing civil law with lots of bosses and at a desk for innumerable hours didn't work for him. Carlos went to work for the Legal Aid Society, an organization devoted to defending the indigents who crowded the city courts. He worked for them for two years, then went out on his own and hung his shingle in Manhattan. For Carlos it was "the best and the worst of times."

For the first time in his life he was experiencing money problems. Passing up the luxuries he had become used to was demeaning, but he had a wife and infant son to support. Living in Manhattan was out of the question. So, despite the belief that civilization didn't exist above 86th Street, the young couple settled for an apartment in the Riverdale section of the Bronx, just north of Manhattan.

But in another sense, it was the happiest time of his life. Peggy was happy to be back in New York, and so was Carlos. They were in love and they had Carlitos, and life was filled with promise.

For the first two years, Carlos never lost a case. He was good and he knew it. Carlos, by his own admission, had a huge ego, something he said you had to have to succeed in criminal law. He found that he could find clients just by going to night court and trolling. People in need of legal counsel would invariably stop and ask if he was an attorney. That he spoke Spanish was an enormous help in signing up clients. At the time there were only three Hispanic attorneys working for the Legal Aid Society.

After six months he stopped being an 18B attorney (listed lawyers who would take assigned clients whom the state paid for) because he was getting all the work he could handle. In the early 1980s, with the crack epidemic in full swing, Carlos became a very busy man. He estimates that 75 percent of his case load was drug-related. Drug dealers almost always paid for attorneys, believing that a court-appointed one could not be very good. Having your own lawyer on retainer was a status symbol, especially among the Colombians who had muscled their way into the drug trade by the early 1980s, and had come to dominate it.

Carlos said that most of the people he represented were guilty, and that was to become part of the internal struggle he would increasingly have to deal with. But, he says, that was the way the system was designed and, most important, that was how he supported himself and family, which was his number-one priority. Defending guilty clients, Carlos developed a way he could turn off his feelings. He had to do it a lot.

Carlos, to balance his city life, bought a house in rural Delaware County. By then another baby, Merced, had been born, and he wanted the children to have a place they could "run around in." But after a few years of long drives to the country, he and his wife thought they should try to find a happy medium. They wanted a place close to the city, but suburban and safe, and most important, a good school system to which they could send their kids.

Peggy didn't like Chappaqua at first, but Carlos persuaded her to reconsider. They bought their first house there in 1987, a modest home by town standards. But the five-bedroom colonial worked well for the family, and, to Carlos' delight, even had a basketball court out back.

CHAPTER FIVE:

THE DREAM TURNS SOUR

IT WASN'T UNTIL he had put in fifteen years on the job that Carlos found himself dreading his work. There were a lot of reasons. Among them, he found that his clientele had changed. They didn't appreciate the hard work that went into winning, and when he lost, all the blame was heaped on him. He also spending more and more of his time trying to collect his fees, rather than practicing law.

Carlos admitted that the law was never his life; it would always take a back seat to his family. That appears to be an understatement, at least according to the later judgment of the Disciplinary Committee for the First Department of the Appellate Division of the New York State Supreme Court.

Carlos got sick with Lyme disease in 1989. In those early years of what many in public health considered an epidemic, there was still little known about the disease or how it could be diagnosed and treated. Carlos said he underwent every therapy known to man. "You name it, I got it," he related.

Because of his reluctance to see a doctor, he suffered under the effects of the disease for seven or eight months before he finally acquiesced to his wife's wishes and had it diagnosed. What followed was a steady regimen of antibiotics. His chemical balance fell victim to the drug therapy and had him slipping into depression. He was put on the new wonder drug Prozac to combat his mental malaise. If anything, the drug worsened his condition to the point of collapse when Peggy had to get him to a hospital for emergency care. Carlos was out of work for two months.

It was a horrible experience. He lost his confidence and felt mired in the depths of his depression. There seemed to be no cure for what ailed him. But somehow he just snapped out of it with the drug therapy he was put on.

One of the problems that the depression brought on was an intolerance for the brutal weather in the Northeast. He remembers telling Peggy that if he didn't get away, the weather would kill him. So, with his wife's consent, the family returned to Puerto Rico. Carlos was also hoping to recapture the love of his work that he sensed he was losing in New York.

They had had a daughter named Alysia by now. Carlitos was the only family member other than Carlos who spoke some Spanish, and he did not speak it well. Merced flat out refused to learn the language. The middle child believed that if he learned the language, he would be doomed to the island for life. Alysia's inability to speak Spanish was Carlos' fault. He admitted it was easier speaking English around the house.

While in Puerto Rico, Carlos had the opportunity to do some work for the FBI in order to get leniency for a client who was under indictment in federal court. He wound up getting far more involved than he had planned. The feds were trying to make a money-laundering case, but they needed a bagman. Carlos fit the bill nicely.

His work for the feds brought him to Venezuela, where sums up to $500,000 in cash had to be delivered and then run across the unguarded border with Colombia. That was the easy part. Getting it out of the United States and into Puerto Rico was the risky part. Through his work as a middleman, arrests and enemies were made. It became another good reason to return to New York.

And so Puerto Rico became a failed experiment for the hopelessly American family. Peggy still hated it, and the kids quickly followed suit. Carlos himself had to admit his ancestral homeland was not to his liking either. He found the island "restrictive." It seemed like all they could do for fun was go out to dinner and lie on the beach, which sounds good, said Carlos, but gets "tiresome" in a hurry.

So in 1999, after three years in Puerto Rico, they returned to Chappaqua, this time for good. Carlos had once again slipped into depression. Peggy knew they had a support system of friends and family in the New York metro area, and New York was where they belonged.

They initially stayed with friends, and for a month Carlos searched for work. He was determined not to return to law, and looked for corporate work. Carlos had several interviews, but was unable to land a job. Carlos was 50 years old and had no real corporate experience.

Carlos was asked to be a co-counsel with a lawyer friend of his, and despite his distaste for what it entailed, the money was good, so he accepted the offer. He quickly picked up another case, and after that another. Before he knew it, he was back in the thick of criminal jurisprudence in New York, a place that kept criminal lawyers busy.

Carlos recognized the obvious. The only way he could make a decent living and afford to live in Chappaqua was to do what he knew, even though the work had become tedious. Once again he found himself handling cases for drug offenders. They were the only felons who could afford lawyers, and they were mostly guilty as charged. Not that Carlos cared. In fact, that made it easier, since most of his clients took the plea deals that Carlos had arranged. Still, Carlos went to trial frequently, more than his colleagues, he said. Sucking it up, Carlos pressed ahead. He believed if he worked hard, in four or five years he could get out for good. His kids would be done with their schooling and he and Peggy would have the freedom to do as they pleased, something they both looked forward to.

Many of the cases he was handling were federal, and had him traveling to Florida or Alaska. He was in demand because, as one of the few Hispanic attorneys who spoke Spanish, he also had a lot of experience representing drug traffickers in federal court. In one big case, Carlos had gotten his client a dismissal. That kind of success got people's attention and made him busier still. The work was demanding, and it kept him away from his family.

For almost two years Carlos spent three weeks out of the month in Tennessee. He explained that the state had become the crossroads of the drug trade. The city of Memphis was a central hub, where a good deal of the illicit product flowed through in its northern march to the major urban centers above the Mason-Dixon Line.

The Perez-Olivo family lived like nomads. First they stayed at a local hotel for a month; then with friends who could take them in; then a series of apartment rentals on a temporary basis.

Carlos believes one of the reasons he got into trouble with the legal policing authority, years later, was his billing practice. He considers himself to be somewhat of a dinosaur in that respect. When he had a potential client, he would study the case, then determine how much of a demand on his time it would be, the seriousness of the charges and what effect it could have on the client. He then would quote a fee.

Professionally and financially, by all appearances, Carlos was quite successful. But the times had changed, and so did his clientele.

For one thing, Carlos was getting more complaints filed with the ethics committee from angry clients who thought that if they paid a lawyer, they would get off. It was an immigrant mentality, says Carlos, that hearkened back to their homelands, where paying off public officials was the way you got things done. To make matters worse, advocate groups encouraged minorities to file complaints for even the most trivial of perceived wrongs, Carlos related.

Carlos never took in retainers. He claimed the reason for that was "a Hispanic thing."

"You come to me," he explained, "and I make you sign an agreement [the retainer]; that's like saying, 'I don't trust your word, so I need this on paper.' That was my logic."

The ethics committee, however, frowned upon lawyers who didn't have retainer agreements. Eventually it would become required, but it was a stick in their hand when it came to Carlos.

Another practice common with his colleagues that he eschewed was hourly rates. To Carlos, hourly rates were just an excuse for the lawyer to drag his feet and pad his bill. But the thing that really bothered him was that the ethics committee never seemed to go after the big firms that were the greatest abusers of hourly billing. They chastised Carlos for including travel time in his billing structure, never showing the same zeal when big firms did the same. For Carlos, it was just another reason to get out of the law business once and for all. Getting out of Chappaqua and back into the city was also in the cards.

CHAPTER SIX:

NEW YORK, NEW YORK/BORROWED TIME

PEGGY WANTED TO live in New York City only once their youngest, Alysia, finished up her senior year at Chappaqua's Horace Greeley High School. It was an understandable decision. Greeley was one of the best high schools in the country—#46 according to *U.S. News & World Report*, December 2008.

Like her husband, Peggy had no desire to return to her roots: she hated the thought of going back to provincial Lexington, Kentucky, and he hated the prospect of being stuck in backwater Puerto Rico, where the only things to do were going to the beach and dining out. Marie knew that her sister did not like living in Puerto Rico because she felt "suppressed" by the dominant male society. New York was the place.

But the expense of living in the city was an issue. "We were similar in so many ways," Carlos explained about his marriage. "I was horrible with money. I could make it, but just couldn't hold on to it. She was worse!"

As a result, the Perez-Olivo family lived their lives on the edge financially. The money went out as fast as it came in. It didn't help that Peggy was a compulsive shopper.

"She would buy stuff and then offer to take it back—something I never took her up on. She knew me well enough to know that I would never tell her to take it back," Carlos said.

Peggy had always felt bad about the fact that she hadn't been productive. Most women in town, it seemed, had careers outside of the home.

In 1999, upon their return to Chappaqua, Peggy had gotten a job as a teacher's aide in the public school system. It was the same school, the Douglas G. Grafflin Elementary School, that Alysia would be attending, and for that reason Peggy applied and got the job.

Then a funny thing happened: according to her husband, Peggy "really liked the work." For the first time in her life, aside from raising her three kids, she felt like she was doing something meaningful. Carlos was proud of her, but most important to him, he claims, was that his wife was happy doing what she wanted.

Peggy wrote her kid sister Marie about her teaching job at the local grammar school. She told her about the special-needs kids she was responsible for and the teachers she assisted.

"She loved her job," Marie said. "She found a lot of personal fulfillment in the work. She seemed to have finally found her niche in life, and she was loving it."

Carlos and Peggy decided to find a house in the suburbs for the sake of the kids. The dream of living in the city would have to wait until the children had grown up and moved out. The family relocated several times, living in a series of apartments until 2000, when they found a house they both liked.

Carlos entered into an arrangement with the landlord that stated in a contract that he would buy the house at a set price after three years, and that part of the rent money would go towards the purchase price. When the lease ended, however, Carlos says the owner reneged because the real estate market had inflated the price he could get for it on the open market.

Carlos sued and settled out of court. He got his "rent" money back, plus an additional $50,000.

Carlos had negotiated an oil deal with some Venezuelan businessmen who were in need of an American citizen who moved freely between the two countries, and it was reaping him $20,000 a month. The deal was something Carlos put together to attract venture capitalists in the States. For his efforts, he was also rewarded with a 5 percent interest in the company, which was located in the Lake Maracaibo oil region. The plan was to buy used oil, clean it ("cook it, actually," Carlos said) and then sell it to the poorer nations of Central and South America.

Carlos claims that money was not a problem. He was able to pay the $5,500 a month rent, and keep up with the car payments for five vehicles and the day-to-day costs of living in a very expensive community. There was even money for trips abroad. For the first time in a long time, Carlos was genuinely happy.

CHAPTER SEVEN:

THE DARK SIDE OF THE LAW

"Carlos Perez-Olivo was a lawyer with an intimate appreciation for the dark side of the law."
—*The New York Times*, November 21, 2006

THE EASTERN NEW York Correctional Facility, located in Napanoch, Ulster County, is one of New York State's fifteen maximum-security penitentiaries. Anthony Stevens is one of 1,190 sentenced felons currently incarcerated in the 100-year-old prison. Stevens, who has been in two other "max" prisons, says Eastern is the best of the lot. It is an "honor stir," where inmates are allowed more freedoms, since they have shown themselves to be less violent and more cooperative with the guards than others in maximum-security lock-ups.

From its façade, Eastern looks to be your stereotypical prison. It's as if it had been designed by a Hollywood film director. The sterile, imposing facility is surrounded by shining chain-link fences topped with razor wire that reflects the sun's rays with an eye-wincing intensity. The prison is nestled amidst forest-covered mountains that form a backdrop that clashes eerily with the massive stone edifice.

The surrounding countryside is some of the prettiest the State of New York has to offer. Just a few miles down the road from Eastern are two state parks known for their panoramic beauty, as well as the Mohonk Preserve, one of the Northeast's most famous recreation areas. Also the prison is just 70 miles northwest of New York City, the urban jungle that gave birth to most of the 1,100 inmates of Eastern.

Stevens, 42, is a smiling, friendly sort, and easy to like. He is articulate and bright, but he has an air of the streets about him.

As he tells it, he is unjustly imprisoned in Eastern; a common lament among prison populations everywhere. It was a bogus rap that landed him behind bars, he says. He claims to be a college graduate and formerly a man of property. Stevens says it was his dabbling in drugs that got him into trouble. From a good job as a road technician for rock groups, Stevens was reduced to day-laboring because he was always partying. He swears it was just the pot and alcohol, and an occasional line of coke. Stevens says he steered clear of the dangerously addictive crack and heroin. His day-laboring acquaintance, "Frank," was the one who got him mixed up with the Empire State's criminal justice system.

He says his present predicament is a result of looking for some extra work with Frank during the holidays in some of the residential high-rises on Manhattan's swank Upper East Side back in 2005. Frank brought him to one building where they collected garbage for removal. Frank said he knew the super, and they would be paid later. Two weeks later, Stevens was picked up by two NYPD detectives who, he said, roughed him up, then arrested him for burglary. Stevens claims he was not informed of his Miranda rights by the arresting officers.

The cops showed Stevens a photograph of him and Frank taken by security cameras inside the burglarized apartment building. Frank, according to Stevens, had been casing the building unbeknownst to Stevens, and later returned to steal. Caught, Frank gave up Stevens and copped a plea in a deal where, in exchange for serving just two years, he fingered Stevens as his cohort in a string of unsolved burglaries. Stevens claims he was then tricked by the detectives into signing a confession that he was told was just a release form.

While locked up at the Manhattan Detention Complex, colloquially known as "the Tombs," he met Elio Cruz, an Ecuadorian immigrant, hotel waiter and father of three. Cruz, 35, was awaiting trial for shooting to death his wife's lover. Cruz had claimed he was innocent of killing his younger rival, German Cabrera, 26 years of age.

The DA's office accused Cruz of following the trysting couple into the subway system and then "assassinating" Cabrera with a bullet to the chest after emerging from a hiding spot on the West 18th Street subway stop. Cabrera died before he could receive medical attention. Cruz was charged with murder in the second degree. His wife refused to identify her husband as the shooter, but the New York County District Attorney's Office claimed to have a very strong circumstantial case against him, including some audiotapes in the possession of Cabrera in which Cruz made telephoned threats to his rival.

Cruz, who didn't speak fluent English, opted to hire a Hispanic lawyer who had a good record of wins in criminal courts. His name was Carlos Perez-Olivo. Cruz raved about his lawyer, and convinced Anthony Stevens to hire him as well.

According to Stevens, after meeting and approving the dapper Puerto Rican counsel, he instructed his wife to pay the lawyer the retainer of $75,000. Half of that amount would be for an appeal in the event he was convicted, and it would be returned if the appeal was not necessary. Perez-Olivo told his new client that there'd be no trouble convincing a jury of Stevens' innocence, calling it "a meatball case." He even claimed he'd make the incarcerated Stevens some money while awaiting trial if he would round up some more business for Perez-Olivo in the client-rich Rikers Island city jail. Perez-Olivo would pay him a 10 percent finder's fee.

Stevens claims he got ten new clients for Perez-Olivo, but never saw a dime of the commissions.

On April 12, 2006, the day his trial was to start, Stevens saw Cruz in the inmate transit area being led away. Cruz hollered to Stevens to fire Carlos, screaming he had gotten "fucked" by the attorney.

As reported in *The New York Times*, Perez-Olivo's handling of the Cruz case was "audacious." In an "unusual episode," a juror had sent a note to the presiding judge stating that she had been "appalled" by Cruz's lawyer, saying she had not been able to sleep because she was so upset about Perez-Olivo's representation of his client. She cited an instance during the trial where the defense attorney was giving his summation and admitted in front of the jury that he'd forgotten what he was going to say.

Elio Cruz was found guilty of murder in the second degree and was sentenced to 15 years to life. He is eligible for parole in 2023. The Cruz family quickly announced that they would appeal the verdict on the basis of incompetent counsel.

Co-counsel Robert Buckley had countered the accusations by claiming that the defense had been "excellent," and suggested that the malcontents had been watching too much TV, saying that maybe they had been expecting "Sam Waterston on *Law & Order* or a *Perry Mason* 'aha' moment." Buckley added that "[Perez-Olivo] handled criminal cases all over the country, and this was only his third loss out of thirty-two wins in criminal cases."

The Legal Aid Society, after looking into Perez-Olivo's defense of Cruz, took on Cruz's appeal, declaring his trial counsel "totally inadequate." As of this writing, the appeal is waiting to be heard, and counsel would not comment on the unresolved case.

The Cruz family also complained to the New York Bar Association that Perez-Olivo had refused to return part of the unused $33,000 retainer. Cruz's sister said Perez-Olivo had promised that he would hire a private detective to investigate the case for $5,000, but never did, and pocketed the money.

For Anthony Stevens it was too late to change attorneys. He quickly found that Perez-Olivo was not the crack defense attorney he claimed to be. Stevens says that Carlos did little during the trial and cross-examined only one witness, even when told by Stevens that witnesses were misstating the facts. Again, Carlos allegedly never hired a private investigator as he had promised.

Anthony Stevens was stunned by Carlos' handling of his case. When pressed to explain himself, Carlos said his bout with Lyme disease had affected his mental faculties and he was having marital problems. In a letter to the Appellate Division, Anthony wrote the following:

> He [Perez-Olivo] also stated that he did things that he shouldn't have done, and didn't do things that he should have in my case as my legal agent, such as file motions, have evidentiary hearings, investigations, cross examine witnesses, call witnesses and object to things that happened in my trial to preserve for the record.

Carlos' summation before the jury lasted just five minutes, and on April 21, 2006, Anthony Stevens was found guilty of burglary in the second degree. The judge sentenced Stevens to the full 15 years, as allowed by the state sentencing guidelines. The first time he is up for parole is 2014. The sentence shocked Stevens. He met murderers in prison who'd gotten lighter sentences than his. Carlos assured him they had a "slam dunk" for a reversal on appeal. Stevens recalls that when he asked Carlos how he could "fuck up his case," Carlos apologized and promised he'd win on appeal. The appeal was never filed, and none of the $75,000 retainer was ever returned.

In a visit to jail by his wife Maria, Anthony learned that Carlos had talked her into investing $40,000 in his Venezuela oil venture. That money came from the sale of their house in Astoria, Queens, which had been put in escrow in Carlos' name for "legal reasons." Carlos had told her not to tell Anthony of her investment, so that they could "surprise him" with a windfall when the oil deal went down.

Stevens asked his wife where the stock certificates for the oil deal were. His wife said not to worry—Carlos was holding them in safe keeping. Stevens worried.

When Anthony asked about the money his wife invested, Carlos said the investment was still secure, but "there were little problems with his wife and his job as an attorney" that were causing delays. Carlos assured him that his problems would all be resolved in a year's time.

Carlos kept in touch with Stevens up until August 2006 when, in the weeks that followed, Carlos stopped taking his phone calls and didn't answer any of his letters. With $205,000 of his money now gone and his house sold, Stevens started looking into legal ways of getting his money and property back.

Stevens did a search of Carlos' oil venture company, P.U.P. Vigue & CIA. The company did not exist. In the meantime Maria got in touch with another lawyer who told her she "could only get the money back if Perez-Olivo renders it to her voluntarily or if she sues in civil court and wins."

On November 20, 2007, Stevens read in the New York *Daily News* that Carlos had been arrested for the murder of his wife. Stevens immediately wrote to the Appellate Division First Department, which oversees disciplinary measures for licensed lawyers in New York City, about his attorney. The disciplinary committee elected not to take any depositions from the convicted felon. They had plenty of other disgruntled clients of Mr. Perez-Olivo who would testify.

There is a problem with Stevens' account of his criminal history, which casts doubt on his recollections of his relationship with Perez-Olivo. Dan Marrone, a former NYPD detective and now private investigator, couldn't understand why a first- or even a second-time offender had gotten such a stiff sentence for the petty crime of burglary—15 years! The usual sentence for a crime of this nature would have drawn 1–3 years maximum. The problem with Stevens, said Marrone, was that everything that came out of his mouth was a lie.

Contrary to what Anthony Stevens said, he, in fact, had

a long criminal record. Most of the crimes were drug-related. Repeat offenders were not afforded much mercy by the New York State penal code. Checks on his academic history drew a blank as well.

When asked by his attorney if he'd ever mentioned having marital problems to Stevens, Carlos burst into laughter.

"Do you think I would ever give a man like that personal information like that?"

As for owing Anthony and his wife Maria any money, Carlos readily agreed that he indeed did, to the tune of $60,000. He had been planning to pay them out around the time he was arrested.

Carlos also concurred that Anthony Stevens was a great jailhouse recruiter of those in need of an attorney, but had never agreed to pay him a commission. What he did do was subtract the "commissions" from the outstanding balance that Carlos said he owed him in legal fees.

CHAPTER EIGHT:

"OUTRAGEOUS PROFESSIONAL CONDUCT"

> *When you hire a lawyer you have the right to have your legal matter handled in a professional and ethical matter. Unfortunately, there may be times when you feel that you have not received the treatment you deserve . . .*

SO BEGINS THE brochure put out by the Departmental Disciplinary Committee, New York State Supreme Court, Appellate Division, First Department. The brochure, much to the chagrin of practicing trial attorneys, is a how-to pamphlet on getting an attorney censured, suspended or disbarred.

The disciplinary committee is made up of sixty-four members: fifty-one are lawyers, the rest are common citizen members. According to the brochure, they are selected for their "knowledge of the law and reputation for integrity and fairness."

After an aggrieved client files a one-page complaint form, it is reviewed by a staff member of the committee. If it is determined that the complaint has merit, it goes through a second screening procedure with the lawyer in question responding to the allegation. Often the committee steps in for "a private informal way to resolve a dispute."

If a case reveals "allegations of serious unethical conduct," the committee has to decide whether to bring formal charges against the lawyer. The formal charges are the first official steps required for public censure, suspension or disbarment.

Gerard M. LaRusso is the chairman of the New York State Bar Association's committee on professional discipline. In an interview with *The New York Times* he said that while every case was different, there was usually an underlying reason for the misuse of client funds: "It could be alcoholism, gambling, other business investments gone bad, matrimonial, depression. I haven't found an incident where the attorney just stole the money because he wanted to steal the money. It's always tied into something."

The court appoints a "referee," acting as a judge, to conduct the hearing, where staff attorneys prosecute the case of the offending lawyer before the referee. The referee issues a "report and recommendation" as to whether the charges were proved, and recommends the appropriate punishment. The report and recommendation is then submitted to the New York State Supreme Court. After reviewing the report and recommendations, a hearing panel, consisting of five committee members—four lawyers, one citizen—is established. If the panel finds the report valid, they pass it on to the court with the appropriate reports and recommendations, which the court will confirm, reject or modify. Only the court has the authority by state law "to impose public discipline on the lawyer."

The first screening process takes roughly four to six weeks. It may not be for another year that the court is ready to determine whether one of the three punishments is applicable here.

In 2006, the year Carlos appeared before the disciplinary committee, they had disbarred twenty-four attorneys, accepted four resignations, suspended thirty-three and censured four.

It didn't look good for Carlos. He wisely sought out some assistance from family friend and lawyer Robert Buckley. Buckley had sat in as the second attorney in many of Carlos' cases. Since Buckley was being groomed for criminal justice by the successful practitioner, helping his friend and mentor was a given. To Buckley this was all a learning experience. Starting all over again in a new career was both daunting and exciting—but he had done it before.

Robert Buckley had been happy with his long career in show business until the ghost of midlife crisis intervened. At the age of 51 his thirty-two-year career on Broadway had finally lost its glamour and challenge.

Buckley had been good at what he did. He had notched up some impressive achievements over the years, including serving as vice president and general manager of the landmark Radio City Music Hall. The aging bachelor believed it was time to move on. He felt he still had some good years left in him, and he didn't want to spend them negotiating contracts with the Screen Actors Guild.

"I wanted to do something dramatic, and if I was to leave show business and silence all my friends who thought I was mad to abandon my career, it had to be [for] something good," he said.

Buckley settled on law. Law requires taking the entrance boards (LSATs) and getting admittance to a law school, then three years of study. That was a tall order for a guy entering a new field of endeavor at an age when most people were considering retirement.

The lifelong New Yorker relates that he had always had an interest in law, and his job on Broadway often had him dealing with legalities, primarily contracts and labor negotiations. Buckley entered Yeshiva University's Cardozo School of Law in Manhattan, where he took an accelerated course of study.

Since he started school in January, he was in a small class of sixty as opposed to the larger fall classes that numbered in the hundreds. Buckley attended all his day classes full-time while still working in the theater business managing a choral group. Because the class size was small, there was a stronger sense of camaraderie and more interaction among the students. Buckley befriended a tall, good-looking guy from the northern suburbs by the name of Carlitos Perez-Hall.

Carlitos explained that Hispanic tradition called for the offspring of a marriage to incorporate the maternal name with the paternal. His mother's name, Hall, was joined with the father's, Perez. Carlitos' mother was an "Anglo," his dad Puerto Rican. "Carlitos" was an affectionate alternative to "Junior," since his dad was Carlos Senior.

Buckley was invited to Carlitos' birthday celebration at a downtown Latino restaurant. It was there where he met Peggy and Carlos. Buckley says they "hit it off immediately."

What impressed the native New Yorker about the elder Carlos was his sense of humor, intelligence and gentleness. Carlos' interests in the arts made him a lively conversationalist and, to Buckley, a man after his own heart. Peggy was a bit modest, but funny, and complemented her husband well, making them a fun pair for Buckley to be around. He was drawn to their enjoyment of the city and love of theater and fine dining. Over the course of the next few years, Buckley was taken into their extended family, attending most of the family get-togethers and holidays.

Buckley recalled that the hearings that would determine Carlos' professional fate were very similar to any court case. They were held in a large conference room set up very much like a courtroom. There was a sitting judge, a stenographer, a referee (prosecutor), defense counsel and a witness box that the aggrieved clients testified from. Carlos would be representing himself. Buckley was there to assist.

CHAPTER NINE:

SUSTAINED

"[Carlos Perez-Olivo] represented the desperate and the violent: not only killers, but also drug dealers, fake doctors and illegal immigrants with minimal resources to pay for their defense"
—*The New York Times*, November 21, 2006

OVER THE COURSE of a year, testimony before the committee would fill eight volumes and 723 pages. There were twenty-eight separate charges (concerning four individuals and one general catchall category).

The committee stated that the purpose of the disciplinary committee's sanctions was not punishment, but rather protection of the public, deterrence of future misconduct, and the safeguarding of the integrity of the legal profession.

Carlos Perez-Olivo was initially charged with disciplinary violations related to his representation of six clients. Because two clients were unable to appear as witnesses—they were in jail—the departmental disciplinary committee withdrew the charges related to them, leaving fourteen charges leveled at Carlos.

Charges One through Seven involved financial misconduct in representing the first of those four criminal cases. Client number one was facing incarceration and deportation, and to fend off state actions, the client's friends and family had paid Perez-Olivo $20,500 to appeal the conviction.

Carlos submitted a "perfunctory application for an adjournment of sentencing and for a new trial." The court ultimately rejected it because it did not have the required supporting memorandum of law or affidavit. His client wound up jailed. Visiting her in the lock-up, Carlos persuaded her to withdraw her appeal to the conviction as "frivolous," then got authorization to file an action challenging the effectiveness of her own trial counsel—i.e., Carlos—at the criminal trial at the "appropriate time."

Despite, or perhaps because of, her legal representation, the incarcerated client was eventually deported. Subsequently the family made repeated requests for at least a partial refund of Carlos' fee and an accounting of how the other monies were spent. According to the committee's findings, Carlos failed to respond to their requests.

Charges Eight through Ten concerned Carlos' involvement in a bail matter for another criminal client. Carlos had been given $10,000 by a sister of the client to pay for her brother's bail, even though there was no signed retainer agreement. The client, an illegal alien, had been arrested in Pennsylvania, where Perez-Olivo was not licensed to practice. Carlos did not inform the client's sister of that nettlesome fact.

Eventually the sister, unhappy with the progress of her case, demanded a refund, which Carlos refused, citing the time he had invested in her brother's case. Carlos did offer to return $2,000, but the sister insisted on the full refund of $10,000.

Counts Eleven through Fourteen, once again, concerned unreturned bail money paid by a third criminal defendant. The defendant's family had sold their home in the Dominican Republic in order to raise $15,000 bail and a $5,000 flat fee for Carlos' legal services, of which half—$2,500—had to be paid up front.

The client eventually pleaded guilty to a negotiated charge. Carlos then persuaded the client's sister to assign the $15,000 bail refund to him on the grounds that he could quickly secure the man's release. He told the family his fee would increase to $7,500, of which he was still owed $5,000. The family was upset by Carlos' latest demand for money, but felt they had no choice except to comply.

Later Carlos refused to repay any of the $15,000. When, in 1996, they continued to press for repayment, they learned that Carlos had relocated to Puerto Rico.

Counts Eighteen, Nineteen and Twenty involved a fourth criminal defendant of Carlos', who had a written retainer agreement with him for the amount of $20,000. Carlos was also representing the client's alleged co-conspirator, who'd paid him $10,000. Carlos, in an effort to legitimize the representation of both of the accused, had gotten waivers from both men to represent them. A district court judge wouldn't allow it and disqualified Carlos from representing the two because of conflict-of-interest issues.

When the second client asked for reimbursement of the money he'd paid to Carlos, he was refused. Carlos claimed he had put twenty-three hours into the case and had the audacity to include research time he'd spent on the conflict-of-interest issue.

The committee also sustained Count Twenty Four, which accused Carlos of having been "engaged in conduct adversely reflecting upon his fitness as a lawyer."

The committee cited earlier admonishments of similar misconduct: neglecting to provide his client an account regarding $10,000 in legal fees, not promptly refunding an unearned fee and failing to cooperate with the lawyer who replaced him.

Another "aggravating factor" was his disbarment in Puerto Rico in 2000. Carlos claimed it had not been because of any malfeasance, but because he'd neglected to pay the required annual fees, and they had no forwarding address for him once he returned to New York. Carlos said it was stupid of him, but in his mind he was never going back, so why bother to pay? He admitted he had a few complaints against him in federal court in Puerto Rico over fees.

In the disbarment investigation, the referee claimed that Carlos never expressed any remorse, saying, ". . . he did not acknowledge the inappropriateness of his conduct nor the importance of protecting his clients' welfare."

To his credit, said the committee, Carlos would agree to

repay the ill-gotten funds if directed by the disciplinary committee. The hearing panel commented that, based on his twenty-five years of experience in law, Carlos should have had the good judgment not to have committed the misconduct reported by the referee.

Throughout the hearings Carlos had claimed it was the aggrieved clients' word against his. Carlos agreed that the heart of the matter was his credibility, and he expressed his belief that it was "unfortunate" that a polygraph had not been allowed in the proceedings. Had it been allowed, he insisted, it would have proved his innocence. Other than being a poorly organized "paperwork guy," he had done nothing wrong.

Carlos also said for the record that he was "a damn good trial attorney," and he had never seen one who was better. As proof of this, the committee was reminded that Carlos had won thirty out of thirty-two homicide cases he had tried before the bench. Assisting attorney Buckley also provided several letters from the respondent's colleagues and judges that attested to his character and his skills as a counsel to the accused.

Carlos' work for the FBI in their investigation of a South American money-laundering scheme by Colombian drug traffickers was brought to the committee's attention.

In lieu of disbarment, counsel Robert Buckley respectfully suggested a punishment that the committee might find suitable and one that Carlos would accept, adding that Carlos was "remorseful and chastened." Public censure and a six-month suspension, Buckley said, would be "appropriate" for the disputed charges brought against the respondent.

The panel was not accommodating. On August 3, 2006, it announced its judgment:

> *The respondent is found guilty by both a referee and a hearing panel of the committee of serious professional misconduct involving dishonesty, deceit, misrepresentation, conversion of client funds, refusal either to return or properly account for client funds*

*in his possession, neglect of a legal matter, using an
illegal "non-refundable" fee retainer agreement, in-
tentionally prejudicing the interests of a client, refus-
ing to return unearned retainers to clients, charging
excessive fees, failure to decline proffered employment that would involve a conflict of interest, and
conduct which adversely reflected upon his fitness as
a lawyer.*

Of the twenty-eight charges, Carlos was found guilty of
thirteen.

Carlos was chided for his lack of remorse and his ex-
ploitation of his "frightened, unsophisticated clients." It
didn't end there.

*His cavalier and disrespectful treatment of the vul-
nerable people who entrusted their vital legal matters
to the respondent epitomizes the very worst behavior
which brings the legal profession into dispute.*

The panel ordered Carlos to pay $10,000 restitution to the
client whose bail money he'd converted for personal use.

Carlos was commanded

*to desist and refrain from the practice of law in any
form, either as a principal or agent, clerk or employee of another; that respondent is forbidden to
appear as an attorney or counselor-at-law before
any court, judge, justice, board, commission or other
public authority; that the respondent is forbidden to
give to another an opinion as to the law or its application or any advice in relation thereto. Respondent
is directed to fully comply with the provisions of Title
22, Section 603.13, of the Rules of the Court.*

Attorney Robert Buckley says he had seen Carlos' enthusiasm for law and his career drain from him. It was because of

the people he was defending, he says. Ninety percent of those clients were guilty and that makes getting up in the morning and going to work and defending them an onerous chore, said Carlos' sometime second.

"The crying and the whining, and . . . 'I didn't say that . . . I don't agree with that . . . Can't you get me better?' It beats you down," Buckley explained. It had gotten so bad that Carlos' stomach would turn on him every morning knowing that he would probably be getting into a heated argument with clients about fees and pleas.

"Because of what he was doing, the element he was dealing with and his sloppy paperwork, all of it conspired against him," Buckley said in retrospect. "To make matters worse, when Carlos got a letter from the disciplinary committee asking for an explanation of a filed complaint against him, his usual reaction was 'Fuck that!' and he'd toss it in the trash."

Carlos knew he was going to be disbarred a year before it happened, since the signs, according to him, were all there. Carlos knew he would have to find something else to do.

Carlos doesn't shirk all responsibility for what happened to him professionally. He knows he was partly at fault. But he was "bitter and upset" about how he had been "screwed over" by the committee. He admits he could have been more diplomatic in dealing with the complaints, but the bottom line was that he just didn't care anymore. He had other financial pursuits.

After the disciplinary committee stripped him of his license to practice law in New York in August 2006, Carlos said he felt that he owed the committee a debt of gratitude. They'd made the decision for him. For the first time, the burden was off his back. He was home more often and not spending nights alone in hotel rooms in places like Memphis. For the first time in a while he was spending time with his family. He was also focused on his various business ventures. And one of them was already paying off.

According to Carlos, his Venezuela oil deal was still paying $20,000 a month in cash, and with a five percent interest in the company, Carlos could envision ample future returns as he looked to attract further investment.

Carlos was also tinkering with raising capital to finance some commercial real estate purchases and buying foreclosed homes for resale when the market dictated. It was now just a matter of getting the venture capitalists interested.

However Carlos' self-professed laziness and his lack of attention to detail would come to haunt him. As Carlos saw it, had he kept better records and insisted on being paid by check, for instance, he might have more aggressively fought his disbarment proceedings. It might have allowed him to take the stand more readily. And it could have gone a long way toward his defense in the murder of his wife.

CHAPTER TEN:

A PEACEFUL COMMUNITY

ROBERT "BOB" BREEN is an affable guy clearly cut out for public relations work, which is a big part of what police work in Chappaqua is all about. Breen would be the first person to admit that the New Castle Police Department (NCPD) is more a service organization than a crime-fighting one. Crime in the wealthy community of 18,000 is a rarity. He can recount the case of an armed robbery, and the one bank robbery they've had in the last twenty years. Memorable in Chappaqua, they were crimes that wouldn't even raise an eyebrow in many of the neighboring communities.

NCPD's style of work is now called "community policing," which includes checking on homes whose families are not in residence and homes with the elderly or sick. All NCPD officers are trained in emergency medical aid.

The most serious crime that the NCPD investigated in any number was burglaries, which is no surprise considering Chappaqua is one of the wealthiest communities in the country. In the 1970s, when the burglary problem reached its zenith, Chappaqua had 200-plus cases reported in one year. In 2007 that number had dropped to thirty.

Breen says his department is one of the best trained in the state, religiously taking advantage of courses offered by the county and state, and the FBI. The fruit of that training is a high clearance rate of investigations.

Breen retired from the department in February 2008 after seventeen years as chief of police and thirty-five years on the force, rising up from the rank of patrolman. A son of a police officer, Breen said he "lived a dream"; he loved police work, and was honored to have served a community like Chappaqua.

In 2006 Breen oversaw a department of forty-two officers. It had been a department of thirty-seven until the Clintons moved into town in 1997, at which point the federal government subsidized the hiring of five more officers who were needed during the remainder of President Clinton's term in office.

The Clintons required a lot of attention from the department. Breen met with the Secret Service every day to learn of the President's and First Lady's movements, since traffic would have to be stopped in both directions for presidential motorcades, which consisted of fifteen vehicles. In overtime alone, the police department racked up $250,000, accommodating and protecting the First Family. The special attention continued after Mr. Clinton's term expired, but at a much reduced cost of manpower and money.

In the thirty-five years he was on the force, there had only been three homicide investigations, the last one being in 1993. Of the three, only one was committed in the town; the other two were a body dump and a murder suspect wanted by another state.

The department detectives rang up a lot of overtime due to the nature of their work. The overtime made it a very desirable position that patrolmen vied for, since the position guaranteed a sizeable jump in salary. Generally there is no test required to become a detective. In most police departments, like the NCPD, it is up to the commanding officer to make the appointment. Marc Simmons was a patrolman when Breen took over as chief in 1991. That year Breen promoted him to detective, then sergeant.

On the night that Carlos Perez-Olivo called 911, the town's four detectives had never worked a homicide investigation.

Bob Breen's telephone rang late on the evening of November 18. He remembers he'd just been watching some TV and contemplating turning in for the night when he took a call from Detective Sergeant Simmons.

"I'm on my way in," Simmons said. "We have got a shooting." Breen recalls his reaction was a shocked "What?" A shooting was virtually unheard of.

"What happened?" he was able to ask after a few moments of bewilderment.

Simmons told his superior that there was a reported possible car-jacking out on Route 100. The victim was at the hospital and his wife had been shot in the head.

Breen got the rest of what was known. The chief told his detective he'd catch up with him later, hung up and got his badge and gun. Once in his car he headed over to the crime scene, just a few miles away from his house. He was on the scene in less than five minutes. There he found Officer Shelby Pellegi searching the shoulder of the quiet highway with her flashlight. Breen helped her get the crime scene secured and did a little inspection of his own of the highway shoulder. He remembers it was pitch black out that evening, without a sliver of moonlight to be had. He didn't find anything of interest by the roadside.

Taking leave of the crime scene, he drove over to Northern Westchester Hospital in the adjoining community of Mount Kisco. Pulling into the emergency entrance, he immediately saw a grey Mitsubishi Montero SUV abutting the loading dock, all four doors wide open. It was 12:50 AM. Detective Gary Beaumont was guarding the vehicle, which had been declared a crime scene.

Upon entering the hospital's emergency room lobby, Breen saw Simmons jotting down some notes in his pocket notepad. Simmons filled him in on what he had learned from Carlos since they had last talked, about the attack by the mysterious gunman. Breen decided to look in on the gunshot victims. He cleared it first with the emergency room doctor, who told him to keep it brief, and, nodding his head, Breen strode into the ER treatment area.

* * *

Flat on his back with his arms folded over his midriff, eyes fixed on the ceiling, lay the figure of Carlos Perez-Olivo. Breen thought at first he was asleep on the examination gurney, but the wounded man was wide awake. Breen was immediately struck by the calm Carlos exuded. It was not what he'd expected to find.

Breen walked up to the patient and introduced himself. He asked if Carlos had been shot and how bad it was. The prostrate man said the wound was not bad, but added, over and over, that this was all his fault. Breen asked if he had driven himself to the hospital after they had been shot. Carlos told him he had.

The chief found it curious that the wounded man never asked about his wife's condition, nor did he mention her at all in their conversation.

"I promise you, Mr. Perez," Chief Breen finally said, "we're going to find out who did this to you and your wife."

Carlos thanked him and said, "You get him."

Breen excused himself and went out to find the ER doctor on duty to ask about Mrs. Perez-Olivo's condition.

The doctor told him her condition was "not good." Breen poked his head in the curtained-off area and saw the unconscious woman surrounded by doctors and nurses, and hooked up to a respirator, IV and other monitors. It was obvious to him that the victim wouldn't be able to talk, so Breen left the room to rejoin Simmons.

"Something is not right here," the perplexed chief said to his detective sergeant.

"Chief, this is so strange," Simmons replied.

According to Carlos, he had been targeted as the culprit by Detective Simmons—to the exclusion of everybody else—from the very beginning.

CHAPTER ELEVEN:

THE CLOSER

SERGEANT DETECTIVE MARC Simmons has a perpetually hoarse voice, the kind one gets from hollering at a ball game all day. But it is the flecks of grey in his black hair that are the only clue to his age.

The New Castle Police Department, while certainly no crime-beleaguered unit, has kept him busy with the upkeep of law and order in a community with demanding residents. The events of November 18, 2006, however, had been a new experience for him; the Perez-Olivo case would be his first homicide investigation, and one that he would lead.

The call came from the on-duty officer who was manning the desk that evening in Chappaqua. Up to that time, it had been a fairly quiet evening.

Simmons was home when the on-duty officer notified him that there were two shooting victims at the Northern Westchester Hospital. The wounded man was claiming that the crime had happened in NCPD's jurisdiction.

After contacting his chief, Simmons then placed calls to Detectives Beaumont and Corrado. He told them to meet him at the department's HQ right away. Beaumont and Simmons then drove together down to the Mount Kisco hospital, arriving at approximately 1 AM.

Assuming the vehicle that was parked askew at the loading area of the hospital's ER was a crime scene, Simmons gave it a cursory search without inspecting inside. He ordered the uniformed officers on the scene to secure the vehicle, then went inside to see the victims.

Walking into the ER, Simmons saw Carlos lying on his back on an examining table. Just beyond Carlos was a curtained-off area where Simmons guessed the other shooting victim lay. From the small crowd of hospital staffers gathered around the unseen victim, he knew the injury must be serious. Simmons introduced himself and Gary Beaumont to Carlos. In all their combined years in Chappaqua, Simmons and Perez-Olivo had never met.

Simmons described Carlos: "He was lucid and calm, as calm as you could expect to be in a situation like this, where you and your wife had just been shot. He was able to answer some questions I had for him."

Emerging from the ER, Simmons oversaw the removal of the Perez-Olivo vehicle by a tow truck and watched as it was whisked away into the night to a locked and secured impound lot in Chappaqua.

Simmons went back inside and then over to where he believed Mrs. Perez-Olivo was being cared for. She wasn't there. Her clothes, thoughtfully, had been removed and bagged. Simmons took possession of them. It was about that time that the department's patrol unit had discovered the crime scene and notified Simmons. The sergeant detective and Beaumont drove down to the area of Route 100 where Officer Bruce Cathie said they would find them. There was little if no traffic as they headed north. They were at the scene within five minutes.

The crime scene could not be missed. The flashing lights of the squad cars and the floodlights from the town fire trucks could be seen from miles away. The figures of the emergency personnel weaving in and out of the artificially lit scene gave it a surreal look.

Simmons got an update from Officer Cathie, who pointed out the blood droplets and the shell casing. Detective Daniel Corrado was the crime-scene constructionist. He made his measurements and took photographs. The police cut out and removed the bloodied one-foot-square patch of asphalt.

Simmons disputes the defense's contention that Carlos had directed the detectives to the exact location of the crime scene. Simmons says that the exact location where the blood droplets and the brass cartridge shell were found was farther north than the place Carlos identified.

"The actual crime scene wasn't that far from the place Carlos said he was pulled over on, but the area that he brought us to was where the lake shore was farther away from the road. That great distance made it a long throw [of the firearm] to the lake. There also were a lot of trees shielding the lake," Simmons explained.

It was two weeks later that the road checks questioning motorists took place. Simmons explained that the two-week delay was because of the Thanksgiving holiday. If the check had been made at that time, it would have been skewered by the influx of vacationing drivers. A traffic count box set up on the road right after the shooting told them that, on average, three cars a minute from both directions would have passed the crime scene at the hour the shooting took place.

Simmons says the information they got from the road check did not advance the investigation. Simmons does not remember Bob Wright and his wife Trish [not their real names] from Katonah being stopped, as he had claimed. Simmons does, however, remember when Bob Wright came forward the first time, calling the NCPD and giving a brief statement over the phone the week after the murder.

Even though Simmons can quote statistics regarding spousal murder, such as the latest one—2008—where it was found that 87 women out of 157 murdered had died at the hands of their husbands in New York, he says he did not focus on Carlos as the shooter. Simmons says he and his detectives dutifully followed up on all credible tips, including several from Carlos.

"From the outset, Carlos was adamant that one of his disgruntled clients was responsible for his wife's murder. When someone tells you that the first time, it is a plausible explanation of what may have happened. We had no reason not to believe him, since I did not know either of them [the Perez-Olivos]," Simmons said.

It was Gianfranco Gazzola who first made contact with the authorities. He had placed a call to the New Rochelle Police Department and told the desk sergeant how he and his son Mark had seen the murder weapon in Carlos Perez-Olivo's possession at a house that Perez-Olivo was vacating. The desk sergeant recalled the case and whose jurisdiction it was, and placed a call to the NCPD. Christmas 2006 was just a few days away.

After a phone conversation, Sergeant Simmons invited the father and son up for an interview. The pair drove up the next morning.

Gianfranco first spotted the gun in a closet on the floor, said Simmons. The father says it was lying on top of a padded envelope mailer.

When Mark was called in, he quickly identified the gun. Mark said he had not wanted to pick up the strange gun, adhering to the practice of waiting for the owner of the piece to perform the safety checks. Simmons says Gazzola is "an avid gun collector."

In a separate development, one of the tipsters in the case was a former member of the Latin Kings, a Hispanic drug-dealing gang with a penchant for violence. The tipster was now a confidential informant, or "CI," for the FBI. When he came across the tip sheet in his daily review, Simmons contacted the FBI and they arranged a meeting with their CI. After speaking with him, Simmons spoke with his FBI handler. The NCPD detective asked the agent if he was a reliable source for them. He was "right on" for the thing they were investigating, but his Perez-Olivo story had changed since he'd first told the FBI about it. The handler witnessed both versions.

"The agent/handler said the CI's overall reliability, outside of the scope he was currently working on, was not good. His information on the Chappaqua murder wasn't credible," Simmons said.

It was also at about this time that Carlos had told the NCPD detectives that "in his heart," he believed that Elio Cruz was behind the killing of Peggy.

Simmons contacted the upstate prison where Cruz was incarcerated and requested that a prison official ask on his behalf to speak to Cruz. Initially Cruz agreed, but he quickly called back and said he had to speak to his lawyer first. His lawyer, a Legal Aid attorney, insisted that certain questions could not be asked, since they might compromise his appeal. The exchange convinced Simmons that the Legal Aid attorney would be of no help to their case.

Anthony Stevens was another matter. Simmons first interviewed him at the Sing Sing correctional facility after Carlos fingered him as another disgruntled client who could have been behind the revenge shooting of his wife.

"In almost the same sentence, Carlos tells us he [Anthony Stevens] may have a lot of pertinent information on the murder, and oh-by-the-way, Stevens is a pathological liar. So we don't know what to think when we finally interview him at Sing Sing," Simmons remembered.

Stevens, without prompting, started to tell the two cops about his case. Stevens was a "predicate felon" by New York law—in other words, a three-time loser. That, explained Simmons, was why the judge in his case had sentenced him to the full 15 years. Stevens had an interesting and baffling relationship with Carlos.

After his arrest for his third offense, the prosecutor offered Stevens 8 years for a guilty plea. But following Carlos's advice, Stevens decided to fight it in court. Carlos lost, and Stevens got 15 years. How can Stevens be loyal to a man who advised him not to take a deal, and then lost the case in court? Bottom line was just as Carlos had said: Tony Stevens was a pathological liar.

Simmons says they did ask the DA's office to perform some forensic accounting of the Perez-Olivo finances. According to the DA's forensic accountant, Carlos and Peggy were up to their necks in debt. Credit card companies had been calling persistently looking for repayment.

The detectives found a pattern of the couple opening credit card accounts, maxing them out, not paying them and then opening another and doing the same. According to Simmons, the financials showed a couple living beyond their means. In their search they could find no real assets, but Carlos intimated that he had plenty of money in offshore accounts. In retrospect, says Simmons, he was probably telling the truth, because his living expenses were huge. Besides the five cars he paid for, there was the $5,500 rent that was never late, even after Carlos was disbarred.

After the grand jury handed down the indictment on December 20, 2007, and the mechanisms of the trial were put into place, Simmons called Robert Buckley and informed him that a warrant for Carlos' arrest had been issued.

Buckley said he wanted to consult with Carlos as to how he wanted to surrender himself. He called back in minutes and told them Carlos did not have a car and it was okay if they picked him up at their home on Old House Lane.

"It was all very anticlimactic," Simmons remembered. "He was outside on the driveway waiting for us. He said 'Hi,' we said 'Hi.' He asked us to wait a moment so his daughter Alysia wouldn't see him handcuffed, and we honored his request. He had always been cooperative."

CHAPTER TWELVE:

LIE DETECTOR

"[Polygraph screening] is completely without any theoretical foundation and has absolutely no validity . . . the diagnostic value of this type of testing is no more than that of astrology or tea-leaf reading."
—Former Supervisory
Special Agent
Dr. Drew C. Richardson,
FBI Laboratory Division

IN AN ATTEMPT to prove he was being truthful, Carlos had volunteered to be polygraphed on at least two occasions, once in his disbarment hearings and the other in the days after his arrest. Both requests were ignored.

In its basic form, the polygraph has been around for ninety years. William Marston invented the lie detector while at Harvard in 1917. His device just monitored blood pressure. A few years after Marston published his findings, a graduate student at the University of California, Berkeley, came up with a device that, in addition to blood pressure, measured the breathing and perspiration of a subject—hence the name "polygraph," from the Greek for "multiple recording."

The modern-day polygraph has changed little in the last eighty years. It still monitors the same three bodily functions.

Several federal agencies utilize the device to screen applicants for employment, and routinely retest entrenched employees. Among those agencies that use the machine are the FBI, the CIA, the Secret Service, ATF and the DEA. Employees who refuse to take the test can be summarily fired.

It was a date with the polygraph that made linguist George Maschke an authority on the device. He and Gino Scalabrini co-authored the scathing book *The Lie Behind the Lie Detector*. The authors make it abundantly clear in their book what they think of the polygraph:

> *Polygraphy is not science. Like its discredited sister disciplines, phrenology and graphology, it is codified conjecture masquerading as science. Polygraph "testing" is an unstandardizable procedure that is fundamentally dependent on trickery. As such, it can have no scientific validity.*

Maschke, an American, is now a legal translator working in the Netherlands. A linguist with a PhD in Near Eastern languages and cultures, Maschke was applying for a job with the FBI as a special agent in 1995 when he took the mandatory lie detector test. He failed the test on the counterintelligence questions and was rejected for the position. The decorated veteran of the US Army Intelligence Corps was shocked by the results, insisting he didn't lie during the test.

A graduate student at UCLA at the time, he did some research on the machine that had cost him the FBI job. He was surprised by what he learned about the polygraph and the "junk science" it was based on. He also found that what happened to him had happened to a lot of people.

As a result of that research and the people he met on the Internet, he formed 'AntiPolygraph.org' whose tagline is "Learn How to Pass (or Beat) a Polygraph Test." Maschke is upfront about what he wants. On the anti-polygraph website it states:

> *AntiPolygraph.org seeks the complete abolishment of polygraph "testing" from the American workplace. Now that the National Academy of Sciences*

has conducted an exhaustive study and found poly-graph screening to be invalid, and even dangerous to national security, Congress should extend the protections of the 1988 Employee Polygraph Protection Act to all Americans.

The website names some famous spies who passed the polygraph when they came under suspicion. Foremost among them was none other than the infamous CIA Agent Aldrich Ames. Ames is believed to have done more damage to the CIA and the American intelligence community than anybody else in their history. Ted Bundy, one of the most prolific serial killers in US history, passed the polygraph only to go out and kill again.

Although there has not been much research in the area, sociopaths are famous for passing a lie detector test, since a characteristic of a sociopath is the lack of a conscience.

"There's no question that it [polygraph] is unreliable," Maschke says. "There is a broad consensus in the scientific community that it has no scientific basis at all. The only people claiming 98 percent accuracy for the polygraph are the polygraph operators themselves."

The main utility of the polygraph for police, says Maschke, is as an interrogation prop, where investigators have a suspect who fears he/she would fail the lie detector test. Given this scenario, the polygraph can be used to put pressure on the suspect to cooperate in the investigation and possibly to accept a plea bargain.

Many in law enforcement claim that the polygraph is only as good as its operator, which is simply not true, says Maschke. "The polygraph," he says, "is based on simplistic assumptions about human physiology that have no basis in reality."

Maschke says a so-called "good operator" uses deceptive questioning to get results. For instance, the operator will ask relevant questions, such as "Did you shoot John?" Whether you shot John or not, you probably will feel anxious when answering that question, because there is a lot riding on it. Next the operator will ask you what is called a comparison or control question, such as, "Did you ever lie to get out of trouble?" The subject is expected to lie to this kind of question. The operator then compares answers. If you react more strongly to the "Did you shoot John?" question, you fail the test. Conversely, if you react more strongly to the control question "Did you ever lie?" you would pass the test.

"If you think that is overly simplistic," Maschke says, "you are right. It's junk science."

Maschke says the measures taken by the polygraph don't correlate in any way with deception. It measures a reaction of a subject when he/she is asked a question regarding a crime. Just because a subject begins to sweat when asked a question doesn't mean he is guilty. There is no machine, says Maschke, that measures deception. "The polygraph is such a sham that you'd be a fool to take it," he said.

In addition, junk science or not, the polygraph test can be easily fooled.

The key to passing it is to show a stronger reaction to the control questions than to the relevant questions. To increase your reactions you want to do something not visible to the operator. One simple way would be to bite down on one's tongue hard enough to cause pain. Thinking scary thoughts while being asked a control question can throw off the polygraph.

It is common for defense attorneys to hire a polygrapher. The polygraph of a client can be conducted in the lawyer's office under conditions of attorney–client privilege, which means no one will know if the accused fails the test.

But Carlos was a believer, because he had seen the results it had in trials he was involved in.

In some of his cases in federal court in San Juan, the polygraph was an effective tool. Just like in state courts, polygraph test results couldn't be entered in federal court as evidence. It could be introduced, however, if both parties agreed. Carlos had gotten clients off by subjecting them to polygraph tests that they'd passed.

Carlos would advise his clients to take the test only if they were innocent, because if they were guilty, the polygraph would say so. Although he never took one himself, never saw anybody take one, or even saw the machine itself, he was a believer. Like a lot of people who had a little knowledge of the device, he spouted the company line that the polygraph was only as good as the operator—the myth of the polygraph, says George Maschke, and an unfounded claim perpetuated by a legion of polygraphers.

Because of his experience with the polygraph and his burning desire to prove himself innocent of allegations that he was involved with an attack on his wife, Carlos insisted that he be given the test. He wanted to take it for his kids. Carlos hated seeing them bothered constantly by the police. The cops would seek them out—even at school in front of friends—to ask questions about their father. Carlos was especially upset about his youngest's experiences with the New Castle Police Department detectives. Alysia was 18 at the time, and vulnerable. The questioning by police had her often coming home in tears. He thought if he took a lie detector test, he could be eliminated as a suspect and end the police harassment.

The NCPD made excuses, Carlos said, saying their polygrapher was not available. When he persisted in his wish to be tested, he was simply ignored.

Even though the polygraph test results were not admissible as evidence, Carlos believed it could impress a jury if he passed it and if it could be brought to their attention—in other words "leaked out."

One thing that George Maschke said could be applicable to Perez-Olivo:

The polygraph was the last straw a desperate man will grasp at to prove his innocence.

CHAPTER THIRTEEN:

THE "HIRED FORENSICS GUY"

MIKE ARCHER WAS the defense's "hired forensics guy." That sobriquet was how the portly 33-year-old described himself to all those who enquired.

Archer had the education and job background to sustain his professional pursuits, but it was the high-profile 2005 Natalee Holloway case where he made a name for himself in the esoteric world of criminal forensics.

Holloway was the Alabama teen who went missing during a vacation in Aruba and to date has not been found. Archer worked for the defense in the New York civil case against Joran Van der Sloot, the young Dutch man who the media hung the "number-one suspect" tag on in the young girl's mysterious disappearance. The civil case against Van der Sloot was quickly dismissed and to date he has never been charged criminally in the disappearance of the pretty blonde.

The "forensics guy" was there to point out what was obvious to him, that Van der Sloot did not kill Natalee: "Sometimes the lack of evidence is as remarkable as [its] presence. The complete absence of any forensics, no crime scene, no trace evidence, and no body allowed me to conclude Joran Van der Sloot did not kill Natalee."

Archer said that Joran could not have killed Natalee and disposed of her body in the brief window of time he had, and leave no trace. The second theory, that Natalee had overdosed on alcohol and pills, and he'd disposed of the body, was also impossible, because again there was no physical evidence that pointed to that. The theory that Van der Sloot had sold her into white slavery was, to Archer, the most probable explanation, but unproven.

Prior to that infamous case, Archer's bread and butter had been civil cases, mostly dealing with accident reconstructions for insurance clients. But as of late, thanks to the insatiable media coverage of the Holloway case, his services had come into demand in criminal investigations.

The Perez-Olivo case was, in a lot of ways, much like the Holloway case. From the beginning, the media had their bead on Carlos as they had on Van der Sloot in Aruba. Carlos was always described as a "disbarred lawyer," and they invariably showed the video clip of him taking a swing at a reporter who shouted out, "Did you murder your wife?" Then there was the mug shot taken of him upon his arrest. Like most mug shots, it was not the flattering image the defense wanted to portray, but that was out of the hands of the defense and into the less-than-sympathetic ones of the media.

Initially Archer had been engaged by Robert Buckley, the Perez-Olivo family attorney and friend to Carlitos. Archer had written him a letter and attached his résumé along with a note describing some of the scuttlebutt in the crime lab community regarding the Perez-Olivo case that was, he says, "outrageous." Buckley called him immediately after receiving his letter and the two men kept in touch over the next few months.

When it became quickly apparent to Carlos' rookie defense team that they would need help deciphering the vast amount of forensic evidence compiled against their client by the Westchester County District Attorney's office, Archer was called in.

CHAPTER FOURTEEN:

A FAIRLY STABLE FELLOW

ALTHOUGH IRA KORNER had only known Carlos for a year, he considered him to be a good friend. He had met his contemporary at Club Fit in nearby Briarcliff Manor. Club Fit, a sprawling facility that boasted a 10,000-plus membership, was as much a socializing milieu as it was a health spa. It suited Carlos' needs well.

Carlos, now, at 60 years old, an aging gym rat, was, besides playing in pick-up basketball games, looking to develop professional friendships. Ira was a retired teacher of psychology just trying to stay in shape. Carlos seemed interested in the fact that Ira not only practiced psychology but taught it at the college graduate level. Ira immediately took a liking to the smooth-talking attorney, describing Carlos as a "glib and fairly stable fellow."

Outside the basketball hardwoods, Carlos favored the sauna room, where he could relax and engage in conversations with other men his age. Ira found Carlos to be a "character" and a kindred soul, for, like him, Ira was an immigrant. Still, the two men considered themselves to be New Yorkers in every other way.

Ira said the loquacious Puerto Rican was a charming guy with a wide range of interests. Carlos' main interest, besides his family, was making money. He was full of stories about his various professional pursuits, and subtly attempted to interest the semi-retired psychologist in some of his investment opportunities. The 62-year-old Mount Vernon resident made it "very clear" that he was comfortable with his pension from New York City and the income derived from a small private practice he maintained. He had no desire to risk it.

Carlos accepted that, but still cultivated the friendship. The two men often had lunch together, with Carlos always insistent on picking up the check. Carlos had Ira over to his home several times, but Ira never did meet Peggy, although he met and got to know Carlitos and Merced. Ira even had Carlos over to his home for the sacred Jewish celebration of Passover.

Ira, because of his profession, became a sounding board for Carlos and his sons. Without disclosing specifics, he listened to Carlos' troubles and the difficulties his boys were going through. Ira even took evening telephone calls from Merced, who was looking for some counseling.

Carlitos, very tall and good-looking, was having some difficulties as well. Observant of people by nature, Ira found that Carlitos was "an independent, self-sufficient kind of guy." His relationship with his father wasn't as close as Merced's. It seemed Carlitos was keeping his distance from his dad, both professionally and personally. Korner believed Carlitos had fallen under the influence of his newly wedded wife's family, a very common thing to happen to young males. Ira sensed Carlitos' in-laws didn't approve of his father's criminal law practice.

Merced was the opposite. He was very dependent on his dad, and anxiously desirous of his approval, support and love.

Carlos was obsessive about money, and seemed to his psychologist friend to spend most of his waking hours focused on financial matters. His latest money-making ventures were in real estate. Carlos told his friend of the prospect of his buying foreclosed properties here in the United States as investments, buying up commercial real estate in Montreal and also waterfront properties in the oil-rich Lake Maracaibo region of Venezuela.

In the months leading up to the murder, it came as a

surprise to Ira that Carlos was having money troubles. Ira had not seen him at Club Fit for some time. Worried about his friend, he called him at his home. Carlos was evasive about his predicament, but the psychologist was able to get to the underlying problem that Carlos was hiding. He was broke. Carlos couldn't even afford the health club. Ira offered to pay his club dues, but a proud Carlos refused his kind offer.

Contrary to Carlos' assertions of strong family ties, Ira Korner sensed that all was not well in his relations with Peggy's side of the family. Rather than a sympathetic bond tying them together after Peggy's death, the relationship had taken a turn for the worse. Korner said that the Hall family didn't necessarily think that Carlos had murdered their sister, but that because of his law practice and the unsavory people he dealt with, he had inadvertently put Peggy in harm's way.

Ira found out about the murder from a friend at Club Fit. The crime scene was not even a mile away. Thinking that his friend could use some support, he and his wife drove over to Carlos' house on the Monday that Carlos was released from the hospital. Carlos, Ira said, was very depressed and exhausted. To Ira, a psychologist, it was no act.

As Carlos' date with Lady Justice approached, Ira became less and less sure about his innocence, especially after Carlos made a request of him that he say he was Carlos' therapist.

Ira Korner was taken aback. Korner maintained a hard line between his professional and personal lives. It was his belief that a professional received payment for services rendered. Sure, he had helped Carlos and his kids, but that was in the spirit of friendship. He was uncomfortable with what Carlos was asking of him. "Quite simply," Ira related, "it would be dishonest."

Carlos, of course, had his reasons. A visit with his therapist could be held in one of the private rooms off the noisy common area, and a professional visit wouldn't be counted against his limited visits from family.

Ira told Carlos he would think about it. On a return visit to his jailed friend the following week, he told Carlos he couldn't do it. Ethically it was wrong.

Although worried about his kids, Carlos, to Ira's keen eye, appeared optimistic and not terribly worried about the prospect of spending the rest of his life behind bars. He was that sure the jury would find him not guilty. With the trial date looming, Korner spoke to the defense attorney who Carlos had recently hired, Christopher McClure, over the phone. He offered to be a character witness for his friend. McClure thanked him and told him he would get back to him. Ira was never taken up on his offer. Korner got the impression they had wanted him as a professional witness and not just somebody from the gym Carlos palled around with. They knew that professionally he would be unavailable, as per his conversation with Carlos.

There was something about the Perez-Olivo case that troubled Ira Korner. It was what Carlos had mentioned a few months before the shooting death of his wife. In a buoyant state, Carlos had said he was about to strike it big. He would have the money to finance his plan to buy up foreclosed homes and hold them for resale.

Korner did not press him for the details or where the money came from. He didn't want to get immersed in Carlos "shadowy business dealings." As far as he was concerned, some things were better left unknown. Ira Korner's life was simple and he wished it to remain so.

As the months dragged on, his commitment to Carlos' innocence began to wane. That bothered the retired shrink. "We all have sides to us that are not so nice, and certainly Carlos has his share," he said.

But what he knew about the man's character and personality just didn't jibe with his pal being a murderer. Carlos had to be innocent.

CHAPTER FIFTEEN:

A FRIEND IN NEED

FOR FRANK FURILLO, a long-time friend of Carlos, their unlikely bond had been forged in the mid-1960s when they were students together at New York's Columbia University. Frank, an Anglo from New Jersey, was on the football team. Carlos, the pre-law student from Puerto Rico, lived in the same apartment building as Frank and some of his teammates. Carlos tutored a few of them in Spanish, since Columbia University, an Ivy League school, expected its athletes to keep up in class. To Frank and his friends, Carlos was a godsend.

Carlos, said Furillo, had a knack for making friends in different cliques. He had pals among the frat boys, football players and, of course, the "Latins." The Latins, from Mexico, Cuba and Puerto Rico, made up a sizeable chunk of the student body at Columbia, and they looked up to the Americanized Carlos, who moved within the university community with such ease. Good-looking, confident and smart, Carlos was the picture of assured success.

Carlos and Frank rekindled their friendship when Carlos returned to Columbia for his second year of law school. Frank was back to earn a master's degree. Carlos wound up sharing a small one-bedroom apartment on Manhattan's Upper West Side at 119th and Amsterdam Avenue with a teammate friend of Frank's, and during that year they became close.

"We didn't have much money in those days, but there

[were] always the fraternity parties," Furillo said. "And Carlos was always a slick dresser, which opened doors."

When Carlos returned to Puerto Rico for his last year of law school at the University of Puerto Rico, Frank took his place in the apartment.

After getting a master's degree, Frank pursued a career as a metallurgist, and took a job in Indiana. He still kept in touch with Carlos, and became a regular visitor to Carlos' home in San Juan. For Frank, sunny Puerto Rico was a welcome change from the often frigid temperatures of the Midwest. The friendship continued once Peggy arrived on the scene.

"Peggy was really something," Frank recalled. "She was quite the character and had a lot of personality. She was awfully fun to be with, and was a welcome addition to our crowd."

After a few months of dating, Furillo said, Carlos actually got scared because he was so smitten with the lovely brunette. To prove his independence to himself, and his commitment to bachelorhood, he planned a week's getaway with a friend who lived in Guatemala. The little vacation promised to be a fun one, but Carlos found himself spending the whole week pining for Peggy. When he got back, he quickly proposed to her. To his surprise, it was Peggy who wanted to take it slow.

However, living together, marriage by a San Juan judge, and the formal church wedding back in Lexington followed in due course.

Frank attended the wedding in Lexington. He recalls that Peggy wanted to have a good time at her wedding, and not appear to be just like the doll on top of the cake. Feeling prankish, Frank and a couple of his football buddies from Columbia took the room next door to the bridal suite. In jest, they all took turns listening to the walls with empty glass goblets. Peggy and Carlos picked right up on this mischief and clearly made an effort to make it a more spirited and noisy event than it would have been.

"That's the kind of people they were," Furillo said. "No

airs about them. Just real fun-loving people who were in love."

Furillo carefully and diplomatically said that Carlos "enjoyed being away from work."

Furillo knew, due to the nature of Carlos' work, that things were up and down for the criminal trial lawyer. Carlos was very successful in his first few years of trial work in San Juan, with all the drug cases he was handling. He got a good reputation, and new cases were coming in all the time.

According to Furillo, Carlos was very focused when he had a case in front of a judge. It was always an exhausting experience for him. "That was the nature of his work, full of highs and lows," Furillo said.

The former football lineman says that there was this very difficult case that Carlos had that involved multiple charges against a client. The defendant had two previous convictions; a third would put him away for a long time, and he was not a young man. When it went to the jury, Carlos had thought for sure that he had won it. When they returned a guilty verdict, he was crushed.

He believed that, despite the evidence, the jury was prejudiced by his client's previous problems with the law. He was convinced they'd convicted him because of his past and that they never seriously considered the strong evidence presented by Carlos at the trial that exonerated his client.

Disillusioned, Carlos took a hard look at his profession, a profession that he had never had any doubts about, and one he had been groomed for. Furillo said it was then that Carlos knew he couldn't continue in law. He wanted out. But getting out wouldn't be easy. He now had a wife and a growing family to think of. Whatever he decided to do, it would have to be in New York. San Juan had nothing to offer the ambitious young man.

* * *

On the evening of November 18, 2006, Frank was home alone and bored, so he called his friends Carlos and Peggy to see what they were up to. It was 9 PM. He got the voice mail on their cell phone and left a message to call him. They traded messages back and forth until Frank finally reached them at around 10:00 PM. Peggy answered the call.

She said they were on their way back home from an evening in the city where they'd had dinner, caught a movie and done some window-shopping.

"Carlos didn't like to talk on the phone while he drove," Frank said, ". . . so me and Peggy spoke. She was in a good mood, and I could tell she had a few drinks. She was happy. We just chit-chatted and that was it. Nothing out of the ordinary."

The next morning Frank's phone rang early. It was Carlitos, calling from Northern Westchester Hospital in Mount Kisco. The news was bad. His mom and dad had been shot. Not waiting for an explanation, Frank left his home in northern New Jersey as soon as he hung up the phone. He was at his friend's bedside an hour and a half later.

Two of their mutual friends from college were there, as well as Carlos' three kids. Carlos was extremely upset.

Frank remembers that Carlos had said over and over how this was all his fault. He knew that Carlos had received some threats as a result of his work, and immediately thought that one of his disgruntled clients was responsible for what had happened out on Route 100.

Furillo spent the next two weeks at the Perez-Olivo house on Old House Lane lending his support, friendship and protection. He slept at the foot of Carlos' bed and was ready to defend his friend from any threat.

It was a terrible ordeal. Every time they left the house, they had to run the media gauntlet. There was no escaping the reporters, who were virtually camped outside the house. They even followed them around town. It had become a living nightmare.

Furillo knew that Carlos had been having an affair. He even met the woman, Ileana Poole, when she was visiting

Carlos in New York. Despite the young and pretty girlfriend, Frank knew Carlos would never leave Peggy.

"All you had to do was see them together to know they would never separate. The thing with Ileana was more about sex than anything. Yes, they did have some common interests, but nothing he would leave Peggy over."

Frank had chided his friend for being foolish. He had counseled Carlos to think of the ramifications if the kids were to find out, and how it would affect them. The kids were really close to their mother, and it would hurt them as much as it would hurt Peggy.

Frank was positive that the extramarital affair was part of the "Latin thing" of which Carlos was culturally guilty. Frank remembered Carlos telling him that there was the Latin ideal of the "big house–little house," where the man had a wife and a mistress, and how it was normal. The way things were, he said.

"Peggy was loyal. She had stuck with him when times were a lot tougher. They were a team, and they covered for each other," Furillo said. "The thing with Ileana, I think, was that it coincided with Peggy's menopausal loss of interest in sex and Carlos' cash-flow troubles. It just all added up. Ileana was an escape."

Furillo knew of the threats Carlos had received, so the theory of the disgruntled client was entirely plausible to him.

"Carlos was not the kind of a guy to get into a fight with anybody. He was the kind of a guy who would talk his way out of trouble. He didn't have a violent bone in his body. And as for shooting Peggy, there was just no way. Without question, Carlos was innocent."

CHAPTER SIXTEEN:

YOUNG AND HUNGRY

FOR ATTORNEY CHRISTOPHER McClure, it was a huge opportunity. Landing this latest client would go a long way toward establishing a name for himself in the very high-profile and lucrative practice of criminal law. Now all he had to do was find a way to successfully defend the man accused of murdering his wife in the tony, wealthy enclave of Chappaqua, New York. It was by no means a slam dunk.

The district attorney, Janet DiFiore, was crowing to the press that they had a strong case against Mr. Perez-Olivo, and the press was having a field day with it. The fact that the purported perp was Hispanic and his dead wife was an Anglo added to the story: racial cases always got more attention. More than that, Carlos Perez-Olivo was a neighbor of the Clintons. That fact alone explained the attention the media was showering the case with. Every article written about the upcoming case never failed to mention that fact.

The problem, as Chris McClure saw it, was that Carlos had already been tried in the media and found guilty. Just getting a fair jury seated might be impossible. McClure, nevertheless, proceeded with a full supply of confidence that the case could be won.

McClure, 39 years of age, is a Westchester native, having grown up in the town of Hawthorne in the southern end of the county. The southern area is the most urban part, due to its proximity to the city.

Upon earning his law degree from City College of New York, McClure went to work for the Bronx District Attorney. While in the Bronx, McClure started first in the Criminal

Court Bureau, then worked his way up the prestige ladder, getting promoted to the Grand Jury Bureau and finally to the Felony Trial Bureau. He was poised to make advancement to the Gangs Squad when he made a career-changing decision.

McClure says he'd always wanted to be a prosecutor, but he adds, with a touch of melancholy, an assistant district attorney "doesn't make a whole lot of money." McClure would have stayed, except that he and his wife, who was also an ADA in the Bronx, found it too difficult to buy a house and start a family on their meager public service paychecks. The money in the business of law is made in the private sector.

Two fellow attorneys, friends who were expanding their private practice in Westchester, were looking for an associate who had experience in criminal law. It was an opportunity that was too good to turn down. On the plus side, Chris McClure would be back in his hometown, where he had contacts and was known. There was, however, a difficult transition he would have to make.

"The transition demanded a different perspective," said McClure, "but my core philosophy of doing the right thing got me through it, because I really believe that the system should be about dispensing justice: the right verdict, the right plea offer, the right decision. My job as a defense attorney is to make sure the prosecutor meets his burden of proof properly and fairly, whether my client is guilty or not."

Carlos Perez-Olivo and McClure's legal partner, Mark Raisman, had a mutual friend who had inquired about a criminal defense attorney. At that time, Perez-Olivo family friend and attorney Robert Buckley was handling Carlos' legal affairs. Buckley had known all along that an experienced lawyer would eventually have to step in to defend Carlos at trial. Carlos and Buckley knew that, as a convicted murderer, Carlos would most certainly get a sentence that would land him in prison for life. A young aggressive attorney with robust legal skills would be needed. Arrangements were made for McClure and Carlos to meet.

In February 2008, McClure paid a visit to Carlos in the

county jail after Robert Buckley had invited him to meet the accused.

The Westchester County Jail (WCJ) is just four miles north of White Plains in the suburb of Valhalla. That the 598-cell facility is known as Valhalla is a cruel irony, since the namesake is the mythical heaven for the Vikings who die in combat. The jail would never be mistaken as a desirable place to be. Seeing the facility for the first time is a reminder of the wealth of the county and the crime problem it has.

As far as county lock-ups go, Valhalla is massive and state-of-the-art. Built in 1987 at a cost of $68 million, the jail is a 100 million-dollar-a-year operation with 900 uniformed and civilian employees. WCJ houses two types of populations within its walls: sentence inmates and pre-trial inmates. There are approximately 400 sentence inmates, who have been convicted on misdemeanor charges and are serving a year or less—more serious offenders wind up at state institutions after sentencing. However, the WCJ's 1,000 or so pre-trial inmates can be awaiting trial, or aren't able to make bail, for charges that run the gamut from DUI to murder and violating orders of protection.

Inmates all wear orange jumpsuits with "WCDOC" emblazoned in big black block letters on their backs. They can receive family and friends at one of the dozens of four-seat tables in what looks like a cafeteria. The small glass-and-concrete-block rooms that flank two sides of the main receiving area are reserved for the inmates and visiting attorneys. Despite the privacy the small rooms afford, the din of the always-crowded main room is constant.

Carlos had been jailed just a month before. A trial was looming, and it was time to bring in an attorney who would argue Carlos' case.

McClure said the interview with Carlos went well. He had some questions for Carlos as well, and they were answered to his satisfaction. McClure confessed that he was concerned about having a lawyer for a client, particularly a criminal defense lawyer. McClure wanted to know "who would be running the show." Carlos assured him that, though he would expect to assist in his defense, ultimately the strategy and legal decisions would be left to McClure.

Carlos, after interviewing the young attorney, decided to hire McClure right then and there. Carlos knew McClure had never defended against a homicide charge, but gave him points for having been an ADA in the Bronx for five years.

"I wanted a guy who was honest, who would work hard for me and who was hungry," Carlos said.

"Hungry" was probably the most important consideration for Carlos, because he himself had lost that trait and he knew how important it was to a defense attorney.

Carlos liked the way McClure planned to handle the case. That is, don't ask too many questions, don't object too much. "You take what you get of the witness, then get out," Carlos said.

According to Carlos, criminal defense lawyers, after making their point, often follow it up with more questions and confuse the issue. He was assured by McClure that he would not make that mistake, and would try the case just like Carlos would.

The shaven-headed attorney further explained, ". . . that you are at a disadvantage with one set of eyes in the courtroom; you can't watch the jury, you can't look at the witness and you can't look at the judge at the same time."

McClure's practice couldn't afford to have two of its three partners involved in the same case, because there were other cases the practice was handling at the time. Everything would have come to a grinding stop if a partner was taken off his own workload to become the second defense attorney for Perez-Olivo.

Conveniently McClure didn't have to go far to find the help he needed. Rich Portale rented office space from the practice. It was Portale who alerted McClure and his partners to the availability of their current offices. Portale stayed on in a first-floor office while the practice took the second floor.

* * *

At 38 years of age, Richard Portale was doing just what he had meticulously planned for—performing in a courtroom. Portale had left his native Niagara Falls area in upstate New York for this kind of opportunity sixteen years ago. After finishing a live law review, where law students orally interact with their professors to prep for the difficult New York State bar exam at Fordham University School of Law, Portale got involved in the re-election campaign of the charismatic and camera-loving District Attorney Jeanine Pirro in nearby Westchester County.

A former athlete at the University at Buffalo and a member of the United States rugby team, Portale's idea of a law career did not include "pushing paper," but, rather like his athletic career, performing and competing. Once a grateful Pirro was ensconced in office for another four-year term, the newly minted lawyer accepted an offer as an assistant district attorney. The first couple of years he spent working in the mundane motions and appeals divisions. Portale called it a "slow learning curve" in preparing for a career on his feet in front of a jury. By his third year he was cutting his teeth in the narcotics and gangs divisions, where he would get plenty of trial experience. After five years of public service, he was ready to move on.

For Portale, years would pass before he got the opportunity to defend a client in a high-stakes, high-profile homicide case. It all started with a request by friend and colleague Christopher McClure.

Portale was brought aboard the Perez-Olivo defense by McClure in early August 2008. He wished it had been sooner, because there was a mountain of research to be done. Chris had not done a lot from the defense side, since he had quit as an ADA just three and a half years before. As Portale had discovered, there's a huge difference between prosecuting and defending. According to Portale, as a prosecutor you are the director and you work from a script of your own design. As a defender you have to be a lot "craftier" and be able to bounce around more and react quickly. Most important, you have to know the answer to every question you ask. Surprises that can catch a defense attorney flat-footed can be fatal in a trial.

That McClure brought in Richard Portale to assist again showed Carlos that McClure wanted to do "the right thing." Needing the help and getting it spoke volumes to the defendant. And Carlos wasn't saddled with another legal fee, since McClure paid Portale out of his own expenses.

Carlos said he could have afforded a high-profile attorney who charged six-figure sums, but he believed he would be in better hands with the hungry up-and-comer McClure. Carlos had one stipulation: he wanted to give the closing statements, something at which he believed he was very good.

McClure thought that was a bad idea, and told him so. The younger attorney said Carlos' emotions might get in the way and that it might be costly strategically. Later, Carlos and his attorneys would laugh about that prospect; it had become abundantly clear that Carlos would never have been able to keep his cool.

The defense's cooperation with NBC's *Dateline* was ultimately Carlos' decision. He agreed to let the investigative news program film the trial, as well as interview him. McClure and Portale were neutral on the issue of cameras in the courtroom. They claimed it would not affect them one way or the other. But the two young attorneys had to have been secretly ecstatic, since nationwide exposure certainly couldn't hurt their practices.

McClure thought the NBC show might even be beneficial, by getting their side of the story out, since most of the press stories to date had been negative, and fell just short of declaring Carlos guilty of murdering his wife.

CHAPTER SEVENTEEN:

JURY SELECTION

McCLURE WAS LOOKING to seat a smart jury. He wanted a jury that he said "wouldn't allow the district attorney's office to fool them with sleight-of-hand legal tactics," and one that wouldn't render a decision based on an emotional response, but on the facts or the lack thereof."

But McClure understood the reality of jury dynamics: "In a criminal proceeding when you are presumed innocent, frankly, they may say you are, but as an attorney I know that if someone makes an allegation against you, the reality is that you have to disprove it."

In theory, the ADA's purpose is to ensure that justice is done and that a fair and just conviction is gotten—but that does not mean at the expense of all ethical processes. "Putting an innocent man behind bars because you pulled out all the stops and did things underhanded, to me, is a violation of our canon of ethics. The state has to be held to a higher standard. It's their burden to convict you."

There are only two reasons why you go to court, says McClure. "Either the plea offer is so high [stiff for the defendant] that you might as well go to trial because you have so little to lose, or the People's case is so bad that it is an assured win for the defense."

McClure said the prosecution's decision to call Ileana Poole to the stand was not germane to the case, since it was "ancient history." According to McClure, the DA's office knew that the affair had been over at least eighteen months prior to the shooting, and it had no bearing on the murder case. "They just wanted to make him look bad."

"Carlos told them it was over, Ileana told them it was over. Did they [the prosecution] expect her to tell them anything different on the witness stand than what she told them at her home in Georgia when she was first interviewed by the police? Like the disbarment testimony, the People were trying to insinuate what couldn't be said in court because it was already deemed prejudicial."

Another problem with this witness was the taped interview with her conducted by Detective Simmons of the NCPD. The tape was part of the discovery evidence turned over to the defense by the DA's office. A large part of the taped interview was unintelligible. McClure turned it over to an audio expert, who was unable to enhance it significantly, making it totally useless to the defense.

Because of the size of the jury pool, the defense only had fifteen minutes to question each prospective juror. Of the eighty prospective jurors, twenty-four made the cut, and the defense had just twenty minutes to question the bunch and use their peremptory challenges. McClure would exercise that right fifteen times.

McClure felt that the People did not accurately portray Carlos' finances. According to the lead defense attorney, the People wanted to convey to the jury that Carlos was broke and needed the insurance money. They only showed closing statements with small sums of money and not statements that had large sums of money being deposited. "It was extremely misleading," McClure would say.

"We didn't want Carlos convicted because of his past. We wanted a verdict based solely on the facts of the case, and that is why the disbarment proceedings against him were ruled prejudicial."

McClure also pointed out that the standard of proof in a disbarment is much lower than a criminal proceeding.

"By bringing in the disbarment findings you are giving the jury the impression he's already a bad guy and probably guilty of what the prosecution says he is."

CHAPTER EIGHTEEN:

MURDER 101

IT WAS THE day after the seventh anniversary of the 9-11 attacks on the World Trade Center towers. Like that day seven years ago, it was beautiful out: warm, sunny and clear, with just a hint of a breeze in the air. The 9-11 anniversary has quickly become a solemn one to New Yorkers, especially those in the metropolitan area, since most can claim kinship, friendship or knowledge of a victim of the terrorist act. The local papers were filled with stories of that horrific day: the always-expected "Where are they now?" articles, updates on the continuing hunt for Osama bin Laden and the *de rigueur* progress reports on the children of the victims.

There was, however, another story vying for the attention of perpetually busy New Yorkers: the opening day of the trial of Carlos Perez-Olivo. It was the kind of story that grabs the interest of the jaded residents of Gotham and its satellite communities, for it had it all: murder, money, sex. To make it more engaging still, the media never failed to mention that the victim and the accused lived three doors down from the Clintons—arguably the most famous couple in New York.

The murder trial venue for Carlos Perez-Olivo was just fifteen minutes south of Chappaqua in the city of White Plains, the county seat. The Richard Joseph Daronco Westchester County Courthouse is located in the center of the hyperactive city that, according to the latest census figures, is home to only 57,000 by night, but has an estimated weekday population of 250,000. The traffic into the city during the morning rush hour seems to bear out that unusual statistic.

Opened in 2005, the Daronco Westchester County Courthouse (named after a respected long-sitting judge who was murdered by the father of a disgruntled plaintiff) is a handsome but austere concrete building that rises twelve stories from a .8-acre plaza that is lorded over by a larger-than-life statue of Dr. Martin Luther King.

The utilitarian design of the building efficiently organizes the courtrooms around a landscaped open space that forms the physical heart of the complex. The seventy-two-foot-wide grassy green—literally a courtyard—is nearly encircled by floor-to-ceiling glass corridors with direct access to the civil courts, the fourteen criminal courts, and the seven family courts. The courtrooms are bright and expansive, all of which are enhanced by the light beige walls and carpeted floors and the sturdy white oak furniture and gallery pews. The Perez-Olivo trial was conducted on the second floor in Courtroom 203, Judge Barbara G. Zambelli's courtroom.

Barbara Zambelli hails from the racially mixed city of Mount Vernon, which borders the Bronx. By Westchester standards, Mount Vernon is a community rocked by crime, shady politics and deteriorating services and structures. It's a given that Mount Vernon is a tough town that produces some pretty tough characters. Favorite son Denzel Washington epitomizes that toughness: a black male actor who fought his way to the pinnacle of the (mostly white) Hollywood establishment, where he currently reigns as one of the top-earning male leads. Judge Zambelli is another tough customer.

Zambelli started climbing the judicial ladder by slugging it out as a field worker for the Commission on Human Rights in 1973 while studying for her law degree at Pace University. A series of city law positions led to her first county-wide elected post as a County Supreme Judge in 1998, a court where she currently hangs her judicial robes.

Zambelli is not known for her patience. Consequently

the 58-year-old jurist doesn't suffer ill-equipped or unprepared attorneys lightly. With her head cradled in her hand, her expressive face usually negates the need for the sharp barbs aimed at long-winded or clueless counsel. All the attorneys polled who have pleaded their cases in Zambelli's courtroom give her high marks. "Tough but honest" is the most common description heard when asked for their opinion of her. She runs a tight, punctual, no-nonsense courtroom and woe to those who disturb the flow.

Zambelli has shown a slight tilt to the side of the prosecution that endears her to the voters and generally ensures re-election in this wealthy, judicially conservative, law-and-order county. One regular courtroom journalist, when asked for their take on Judge Zambelli, quipped: "Let me put it this way. If I was up on a felony rap, Zambelli is the last judge I'd want to see on the bench."

Westchester County District Attorney Janet DiFiore had taken office in January 2006, succeeding the flamboyant headline-grabber Jeanine Pirro, who'd served a tumultuous twelve years at the White Plains office. Signaling a break with her predecessor, DiFiore never mentioned Pirro's name in the brief five-minute address she gave upon taking office, despite having worked under Pirro as a prosecutor for several years.

Just prior to the start of the trial, on August 17, 2008, DiFiore took another big step in separating herself from the past when she switched party affiliation from Republican to Democrat.

"After careful consideration," DiFiore announced, "I decided to change my party registration because the principles of the Democratic Party are closely aligned with my views."

The 53-year-old became the first Democrat to hold that office in 112 years.

Despite her new party alliance, DiFiore was not soft on crime. One could not be and hope to get re-elected in wealthy, get-tough-on-crime Westchester County. Her split with the past was more style than substance. The DA's office under DiFiore was as aggressive as ever in its pursuit of justice. The prosecution of Carlos Perez-Olivo would be a good example of that prosecuting zeal.

It took two and a half days to select a jury. By all appearances, the jury was the one that both the defense and prosecution said they wanted: "a smart one," according to defense co-counsel Richard Portale, explaining that the trial was going to be a long one, with a lot of forensic evidence to digest.

The twelve jurors and seven alternates consisted of nine white males, one Hispanic man, four white females, two black men and three black females. They were mostly middle-aged and, from stating their professions, were educated and well spoken. They came from all over the county—except from Chappaqua. There had been two prospective jurors in the eighty-man jury pool who'd hailed from the affluent community, but they had been excused because they confessed they were very familiar with the case, having followed it closely, and had already formed the opinion that Carlos Perez-Olivo was guilty of murdering his wife.

On the second day of jury selection, immediately after lunch break, Judge Zambelli heard an appeal by *Dateline NBC* to allow a camera to record the opening and closing statements of the trial. For over a century, cameras of any kind have been banned from New York State courts, but individual county courts could consider appeals for one-time dispensation.

The popular network true crime/mystery show was in production for a one-hour program on the Perez-Olivo murder. No one besides the judge, the attorneys and the NBC duo of producer Sarah Karlson and NBC lawyer Daniel Kummer would be allowed in the courtroom for the fifteen-minute hearing. The appeal was granted. Kummer was evasive when asked what arguments the network had advanced and why Judge Zambelli had acceded to their plea, saying, "I really can't go into details." When pressed about all the secrecy, attorney Kummer further obfuscated in replying, "It's not an issue of 'secrecy,' but rather simply a matter of respect for the court and the process that the judge chose to follow in handling our application and a desire not to do anything to jeopardize the relief that the judge granted."

At precisely 9:30 AM on Friday, September 12, Judge Barbara Zambelli bid jury members a cheery good morning, as she did—by name—to all the attorneys. Lastly Carlos Perez-Olivo was greeted. He was the recipient of her warm smile just like everyone else. Even though she was seemingly brusque in nature, the blonde, bespectacled judge always put on her happy face at the beginning of proceedings. The court clerk, the court reporter, the bailiff and the court officers were all familiar with the judge's MO, and they anticipated nearly all her commands and hopped to the ones that they didn't. Zambelli's courtroom had a well-deserved reputation of being run in a very businesslike fashion.

Prior to opening statements, Zambelli had to hear the special late requests of three jurors for excusal. One by one they took a seat and explained their problems—one health-related, two job-related—with serving as a juror on a case that was expected to run six weeks. Ultimately only one was reluctantly granted, to an irreplaceable emergency room physician whose superior had pled for his excusal to the district attorney.

Assistant District Attorney Christine O'Connor took the podium that faced the jury. She lost no time getting to the main contention of the prosecution, which was that the Perez-Olivos did not have the "perfect marriage." O'Connor said it was "all a veneer," and that Mr. Perez-Olivo was "charming, accomplished and quite capable of hatching and committing this perfect murder." The trial attorney, in her mid-30s, and looking significantly younger, told the nineteen riveted jurors who sat quietly before her that, while on their way home from an evening in the city that had included a movie and dinner, Carlos had taken a circuitous detour and pulled his Mitsubishi Montero SUV to the side of a dark, secluded road and shot his dozing wife of thirty years, execution-style, in the back of the head, then turned the gun on himself and inflicted a superficial wound on his fatty left-side abdominal area.

Why? O'Connor asked rhetorically. According to the assistant district attorney, it was because, having been disbarred from the practice of law three months before the murder, Carlos' career was in a "downward spiral." The ADA said that on November 17, 2006, Carlos had only $400 in his checking account. There was, however, $900,000 worth of life insurance on his wife, an eye-catching amount for a middle-aged teaching assistant who had been earning less than $30,000 a year. O'Connor also revealed that the debonair Puerto Rican native had been carrying on a ten-year affair with a woman twenty-five years his junior.

O'Connor claimed that because Carlos was a criminal defense attorney, he thought that he could get away with killing his wife and be financially rewarded for it by the life insurance policies. The ADA called it "Murder 101." But, said O'Connor, Carlos did not foresee the damning forensic evidence compiled by a consortium of New York state police and investigation units. He'd thought he was "capable of hatching and committing this perfect murder." However, he had not been careful enough.

ADA O'Connor concluded in her forty-five-minute opening statement that the defendant's claim of a "phantom gunman" would be exposed as fabrication by the physical evidence compiled by the prosecution.

CHAPTER NINETEEN:

SEARCH AND RECOVERY

THE DEFENSE'S CASE was articulated by co-defense attorney Christopher McClure. The conservatively dressed 39-year-old contended in his brief fifteen-minute opening that the forensic and ballistic evidence compiled by the DA's office was "inconsistent with the tale the prosecution will tell." McClure said it was "a fairy tale involving only one victim" and their account "is a manufactured and biased interpretation."

The defense counsel also claimed that Carlos' extramarital affair was long over at the time of the murder, that his client was not broke and that the case was handled by "inexperienced detectives, way over their heads." He told the jury that they would also be "appalled and offended" by the 911 respondents, who were more concerned with jurisdiction issues than in sending help to the seriously injured couple, forcing Carlos to drive himself and his mortally wounded wife to the hospital several miles away.

According to the defense, Carlos was fully cooperative with police, and availed himself to investigators whenever requested. That, he said, proved he had nothing to hide.

It was after an hour lunch break on the first day in court that the first witness was called by lead ADA Perry Perrone, head of the homicide division of the DA's office.

Officer Shelby Pellegi is a patrol officer with the New Castle Police Department, and was on duty on the east side of her jurisdiction in Millwood on the night of November 18, 2006. The 38-year-old, seven-year police veteran was directed to investigate an area of a reported shooting along

Route 100 near the Taconic State Parkway, just two miles from her present location. The compact, dark-eyed, dark-haired officer proceeded to canvass the area by slowly driving along the shoulder of the sparsely driven thoroughfare. It was when she was joined by fellow officer Wall that an important discovery was made. The two uniformed police officers simultaneously found blood spatter and a brass shell casing on the highway shoulder.

Defense attorney McClure interrupted Pellegi's testimony several times to object to her use of certain terms. McClure complained to an impatient Judge Zambelli that Officer Pellegi was not a forensic expert, and the defense objected to her use of the words "blood spatter." Zambelli overruled all his objections, but told the testifying officer to refrain from using the term.

Next on the stand was New York State Trooper Christian McCarthy. McCarthy was on the state police scuba team, charged with search and recovery of victims and evidence for the New York State Police and departments across the state that were too small to have their own dive units—the New Castle Police Department among them.

McCarthy, 40, a fourteen-year veteran of the state police, explained to the jury that there was one dive team per troop, making eight teams across the state. Each team consisted of eight divers. Currently, there were sixty-one total active divers. Volunteer divers were regular road troopers who attended dives as needed, and were not full-time. To become a member, you had to pass a three-day try-out, and from there, attend a six-week school, with a 33 percent failure rate.

It was apparent from his witness stand demeanor that he had testified in court many times. Responding to ADA Perrone, McCarthy estimated that he had taken part in over fifty search-and-recovery operations as a ten-year member of the scuba team.

The buzz-cut trooper spoke clearly and evenly about the search for evidence in Echo Lake on the afternoon of November 22, 2006, four days after the murder.

According to McCarthy, police divers had entered the murky water from the western bank of the lake, approximately ten feet from the guardrail that bordered the shoulder of Route 100. It was where a .32-caliber shell casing and blood droplets had been found. The spot, near a cut-out in the guardrail and a fire hydrant, had been marked by a small square of new asphalt that replaced the bloodstained patch removed for lab analysis by forensic experts.

On an aerial photo of the lake that had been set up on an easel before the jury, Trooper McCarthy detailed the dive plan and pointed out various locations of importance, including the spot where he had made the fortuitous discovery for the New Castle Police Department and ultimately the Westchester County District Attorney's office.

The lake, twelve feet deep, had an easily stirred fine silt bottom that McCarthy estimated to be four to five inches deep, and which covered a hard-packed mud base. Due to the zero visibility, McCarthy and his dive buddy blindly worked opposite ends of a 100-foot search line, which they inched along, probing the silt with their neoprene-gloved hands. They were supervised from the shore by the dive team leader, trooper and chief diver Joseph Benzinger.

Just minutes into the search, McCarthy felt a hard rock-like object in the muck. After a few seconds of probing it with his hands, the veteran diver/cop knew he had something of interest. Carefully cradling it in his hands, McCarthy ascended from the bottom. It wasn't until he was on the surface, with most of the silt washed away, that he could see that what he held in his hand was a small-caliber semi-automatic pistol. He gestured to Benzinger that he had something and was coming in.

The handgun was carefully handled, as if it were a fragile piece of china, by McCarthy, who, once reaching the banks, gently handed over the find to dive team chief Benzinger who placed it in a Tupperware container. Benzinger then drew some water from the lake and poured enough in the gun container to forestall electrolysis, which, if not taken into account, would corrode the metal parts of the pistol, rendering it useless as evidence in any investigation. Their job over, Benzinger passed the Tupperware container to Patrol Sergeant James Wilson of the NCPD, who promptly stashed it in a lockbox of his squad car, then drove to police HQ, where he locked the find in the secured property room of the department.

In the cross-examination of McCarthy, defense attorney Chris McClure queried the trooper on the exact location where the gun had been found in the lake. Taking in the distance of the highway shoulder, McClure was able to get the policeman to agree that the gun had been thrown a good fifty feet. Considering the defendant's age—58 at the time of the incident—and the fact that he was wounded, the idea, McClure hinted, that Carlos had thrown the weapon was far-fetched. McClure also was able to cite obstructing trees hampering a successful toss, and the fact that his client had directed police to the spot where the crime happened—incidentally giving the dive team a launching point for their successful underwater search.

Quickly following McCarthy was another uniformed officer, the first responding New Castle policeman. Patrol Officer Ernesto Geraldez, an eight-year veteran of the NCPD, had also been with the White Plains PD seven years prior to his employment in the northern end of the county. Geraldez was one of six officers assigned to the patrol division of the quiet community, a night-and-day difference from the grittier streets of White Plains.

Geraldez testified that he was working the overnight shift at approximately 11:30 PM when he was notified by HQ that the department had received a call from the adjacent Mount Kisco Police Department. They had two gunshot victims at Northern Westchester Hospital. One of the victims claimed to have been shot on Route 100 in Millwood, part of the NCPD jurisdiction. From Chappaqua, Geraldez sped over to the medical center, five miles distant from his patrol location. He arrived ten minutes later.

Geraldez surmised that the grey SUV with all its doors open, which was partially blocking access to the ER, belonged to the victims. He peeked in and saw the bloodstains, but touched nothing.

Inside the emergency room, he found one of the victims, a middle-aged male Hispanic being treated by the ER nurses. Geraldez noted what appeared to be the gunshot wound in the left abdominal area of the victim. He could see the other victim being attended to in another curtained-off area of the ER. The male, he learned, was Carlos Perez-Olivo. Asked by ADA Perrone to point him out in the courtroom, Geraldez fingered the man in the middle of the defense table on the other side of the courtroom as the person in question.

Geraldez was asked by the ADA what had been his first order of business. The policeman explained that he'd had to find out quickly what had happened—he needed a brief description of the perpetrator and the car he was in so an alert could be sent out to the forty-two police departments in the county, as there was allegedly an armed and dangerous suspect on the loose.

Perez-Olivo told the policeman that he and his wife had been returning from a night out in New York City, when they'd been forced off the road onto the shoulder by an older model Toyota Camry. A thirtyish Hispanic man, possibly Colombian, had jumped into the back seat of their SUV and drawn a gun, and a struggle ensued. Shots were fired when Carlos tried to wrestle the gun away from the armed man. Perez-Olivo felt the sting of a bullet and thought the shooter also had been wounded. The shooter lurched out of the SUV then fled into the Camry with two other men.

Assessing the situation, Perez-Olivo realized that his wife had been shot during the in-car melee and was unresponsive. He then dialed 911 on his cell phone and sped off in the direction of the nearest hospital, Northern Westchester.

Carlos told the officer he had taken the Taconic State Parkway and Route 9A home from the city. Noting their address in the eastern part of town, Geraldez asked why he hadn't taken the Saw Mill River Parkway home, as it was a more direct route to Old House Road, just three minutes from the Saw Mill exit. Carlos said he'd intended to get gas for his car, and knew the Exxon station at the intersection of Route 100 and Campfire Road was open 24/7. Geraldez told the court that there were also all-night gas stations close to the Saw Mill exit and near the Perez-Olivo residence.

Carlos told his fellow Puerto Rican that he didn't believe the assault was random. Because of his law practice, he said he had many enemies and there had been many threats to his life.

After the lunch break, the prosecution called their key witness, the man who ultimately would make or break the case. They were showing their hand early and had court watchers doubting the trial would last the six weeks originally projected. His name, one unknown to the media up to this point, was Mark Gazzola.

Gazzola was by all appearances, and in fact is, a thirty-something Italian-American blue-collar worker. Mark was the nephew of Mario Gazzola, who owned the house on Devoe Road where the Perez-Olivos resided in June of 2006, before moving to Old House Lane. ADA Perry Perrone made sure the jury understood it was just five months before the fatal night on the deserted road in nearby Millwood.

It was obvious from the start that Gazzola was the kind of witness prosecutors dream about having testify for them. He was handsome, blue-collar, impatient—no doubt his civic duty meant wages lost—and, being the good citizen that he was, had come forward on his own accord. He also addressed the jury loud and clear, without so much as an "uh" in the testimony. But best of all—Gazzola was a gun nut.

At the prompting of Perrone, Gazzola told the jury of his lifelong passion for guns: membership in the NRA, the frequent trips to the pistol range, his position as a gun safety instructor and his multi-gun collection. He was quick to add he was no "expert," but he was very familiar with all aspects of guns and gun collecting.

According to his testimony, Gazzola had been contacted by his uncle, who was traveling abroad and desperately needed someone to clean up a vacant rental property that he had recently sold. Mark told his uncle he would help, and proceeded to drive north from his home in the Bronx to the wealthy enclave of Chappaqua. When he arrived at the house on Devoe Road, Carlos, Peggy and their teenage daughter, Alysia were still there packing. The house was supposed to be empty, and the place was a mess. Mark Gazzola told his uncle in an international phone call that Mark would have to call in his dad Gianfranco, to give him a hand in cleaning up the house.

Mark's father joined him, and not long after starting the clean-up, Mark heard his dad holler for him from a second-floor bedroom. Upstairs, he found his dad in the closet of the bedroom, staring down at the contents of a small box. Looking up to his son, the elder Gazzola said, "You're the expert, what do we have here?"

Mark knew exactly what it was upon seeing it. It was a handgun, and a very desirable one among collectors—one that he had coveted for a while, a Walther PPK .32-caliber semi-automatic.

The German-made prewar pistol was known as the "James Bond gun," as the fictional British super-spy, 007, with "a license to kill," favored the easily concealed handgun. Throw into the mix its literary/cinematic notoriety, and you had a collectible hard to find and usually quite expensive— over $1,000 in today's market. Mark called down and asked Carlos to come upstairs.

When Carlos appeared in the room, Mark told him that he had forgotten something, gesturing toward the open box on the floor of the closet. Mark, thinking it might lead to a dream purchase, drew Carlos into a conversation about the handgun. After some friendly banter, Mark finally asked the Chappaqua attorney if he would consider selling the "Bond" gun. Carlos said no. The gun, he explained, was a gift that had sentimental value and he couldn't possibly part with it. Mark told the jury that he'd been disappointed, but understood Carlos' sentiment: if it had been Mark's, he wouldn't sell it either, not for any price.

Up until November 19, Mark Gazzola had forgotten all about the gun. He began to studiously follow the case in the ensuing weeks, telling family and friends that if he found out that the weapon used was a .32-caliber handgun, he would feel compelled to report his discovery to police. When he learned that it was in fact a .32-caliber bullet that had killed Mrs. Perez-Olivo, Mark knew he would have to come forward.

In their cross-examination, McClure repeatedly hit home on the fact that Gazzola was no expert in the field of handguns. Exasperated by McClure's persistence and the tone of his questioning, Gazzola did say that even though he was not a "trained expert," he had picked up a thing or two on guns over the years. He steadfastly insisted that the gun in the evidence bag in front of him was the same one he had seen at his uncle's property in the possession of his tenant, Carlos Perez-Olivo, five months before the murder of Peggy.

After Mark left the stand, Detective Arthur Holzman became the last witness of the day. Holzman, a ballistic expert with the Westchester County crime lab, related how he'd retrieved the two spent bullets and three shell casings from the Mitsubishi Montero. From his experience he also testified that bullets "do strange things," and might not leave a mark on asphalt after striking it. This would play into the prosecution's contention that Carlos had shot himself outside of the vehicle near where the blood droplets and shell casing were found, and would also explain why the third bullet had not been found. Holzman would continue his testimony the following Monday.

On the second day of trial, two nurses followed the

ballistic expert to the stand. Carol Collins told the court that while on the way to work, she had been passed by the speeding Montero at a traffic light near the hospital. When she arrived at her place of employment, she saw the same Montero parked erratically at the ambulance entrance to the ER. She and two others had removed the unresponsive victim from the front passenger's seat and had seen her into the treatment area.

Shelly Griesinger was the ER nurse on duty the night of November 18. She told the court that Carlos had been insistent that his wife be treated first and, echoing Collins, Carlos had seemed genuinely distraught by the events of the evening. The defense stressed that point in cross-examination.

Next up was NCPD Sergeant Bruce Cathie, the supervising patrol officer and a responding officer who'd followed Geraldez to the hospital the night of November 18. Cathie was the one who'd taken the call from the Mount Kisco PD, and had sent first responder Geraldez ahead. Cathie'd left HQ shortly after, and joined Geraldez at the hospital, where he questioned the wounded man as well.

The prosecution was able to elicit from the fourteen-year veteran cop that Perez-Olivo's route home didn't make much sense. Also, Cathie expressed puzzlement as to why the victims had been so far south on Route 100 when the crime occurred. Why, if they had been on the Taconic Parkway like Mr. Perez-Olivo said, hadn't he exited at Campfire Road? Using the aerial photo of the area, the police sergeant showed the jury the location of the gas station and the logical and nearest exit to the station that the couple could have taken. The crime-scene location was almost a mile south in a dark and quiet stretch of the lightly traveled road.

Cathie also told the jury about inspecting the crime scene with officer Pellegi that evening after leaving the hospital. It was then that he and Pellegi had found the blood droplets and the gun shell casing. But, he said, in response to ADA Perrone's question, they'd found no skid marks or signs of an abrupt stop or crash that would bolster Carlos' contention that he was forced off the road by the unknown assailant. Again, in cross, Perez-Olivo attorney McClure reaffirmed that it was his client who had directed the cops to the crime scene.

CHAPTER TWENTY:

THE OTHER WOMAN

AFTER THE LUNCH break, some of the media reporters had not returned from lunch when the prosecution called Ileana Poole to the stand.

The newspapers and television reporters had been expecting the woman to testify—but not so soon, hence their absence. Poole was the witness who would sell newspapers and have TV viewers put down their remotes—the striking, dark-eyed beauty was the 35-year-old mistress of the accused.

Wearing a dark skirt and jacket over a white blouse, Poole sat as still as a statue, eyes focused in the direction of ADA Christine O'Connor, her questioner, who stood at a podium directly in front of the witness box. Poole's eyes never wandered, no doubt for fear of making contact with her former lover or the accusing eyes of the jury. It was readily apparent that the woman would rather have been any place else than here. Her shame for airing her adulterous behavior in an open courtroom was palpable. Many of the jurors could be seen shifting uncomfortably in their seats.

ADA O'Connor was uncharacteristically deferential to the witness. It was not the usual tone she affected for the jury, but a soft sympathetic one. It was a toss-up who was more uncomfortable with the line of questioning, the defendant's mistress or the prosecuting attorney.

Ileana Poole—then Ileana Santana—testified that she'd met Carlos when she worked in a children's shoe store in San Juan, Puerto Rico, in 1993, when she was just 21 years old and single. Carlos was 44 and married. He'd been shopping for shoes for his daughter and was immediately smitten by the statuesque beauty of the salesgirl. According to Poole, their conversation lasted several minutes. The next day flowers for her arrived at the store, followed by a phone call and an invitation to dinner. The impressionable young girl accepted, and so began an on-again, off-again affair with a man almost twenty-five years her senior, that would play out for the next fifteen years. According to her testimony, the last time she could recall speaking with him was on her birthday, November 18, 2006, the day of the murder.

Poole said the two lovers would rendezvous in Puerto Rico, New York City, Montreal and Atlanta, where Ileana now lived with her husband and small child. The physical nature of their relationship, Ileana claimed, had ended sometime in 2003, but the pair had remained friends and often spoke over the phone.

ADA O'Connor ended her questioning by asking if Poole's trip to New York and her hotel and expenses had been paid by the Westchester DA's office. Poole said they were.

The defense, who had tried unsuccessfully to suppress the evidence of an affair as prejudicial to their client, tried to hammer home that the love affair had been long over by the evening of Peggy's murder. Ileana confirmed that fact.

Before being excused, there was some chatter among counsel and the judge about the quality of a tape made by Detective Simmons during his interview with Poole that had been turned over to the defense in the discovery phase. The defense wanted to question Poole about it, since they said it was of poor quality. Judge Zambelli nodded her head and then gave Poole the bad news that she would have to return to the stand to give more testimony. That meant two more overnights, since Tuesdays were Judge Zambelli's "duty" day, and a day off for the jury.

Poole looked as if she would break into tears. Carlos called over his attorneys for a few words. In hushed tones, he told his lawyers to let her go, that she'd been through enough.

Breaking the huddle, McClure announced to the judge that the defense waived their right to question the sitting witness further. Zambelli turned to the distraught witness and told her she was excused. Somewhat stunned, Poole wasted no time in exiting the building without so much as a passing glance toward her former lover, the accused.

Finishing up the day in court was NCPD Detective Sergeant James Wilson, the supervisor for the department's three detectives. He had joined the uniformed officers in their early morning search on November 19 after being called in by his chief. Wilson had also been the detective on duty on November 22 when the underwater search and recovery of the handgun was made by the state police dive team. Step by step he detailed his careful handling of the purported murder weapon, which was shaping up to be the key piece of evidence in the prosecution's case.

CHAPTER TWENTY-ONE:

RECONSTRUCTION AT THE CRIME SCENE

ON WEDNESDAY, SEPTEMBER 17, 2008, just three witnesses would take the stand. First was Diane Crisalli, a teacher friend of Peggy Perez-Olivo. The prosecution tried to get the fact across that the murder victim made little as a teacher's assistant at Chappaqua's Douglas G. Grafflin Elementary School. ADA Perrone was effectively stymied by the defense's objections to her remarks about Peggy's salary as hearsay, but nevertheless was able to convey to the jury that it was less than $30,000 a year.

Next up was Eric Hartman, the security head of the hospital, who explained the fifty-seven-camera video surveillance system. Hartman then described to the court what they were watching on the monitor when the tapes from the ER cameras, on the evening of November 18, 2006, were shown. The staccato-action videos followed the Perez-Olivos SUV's arrival at the hospital's ER ambulance stand. Carlos was then seen walking up to the admitting station, standing without assistance and then being brought by a wheelchair into the treatment area. There was a brief glimpse of the prone figure of a motionless Peggy being wheeled into the treatment area. The gravity of Carlos' wound was subtly called into question, especially juxtaposed against Peggy's seemingly dire condition.

Lieutenant Detective Marc Simmons was a key witness for the DA's case. He was the chief detective for the NCPD and the lead investigator in the Perez-Olivo homicide. A boyish-looking 42-year-old, Simmons had served a total of twenty years in the department, though in all those years he had investigated just one other homicide.

Simmons was a hands-on detective, not just an administrator. He carried his own load of cases. The lieutenant detective had had plenty of training, just not a lot of practical experience. The town of New Castle encompassed the villages of Chappaqua and Millwood. Investigating burglaries, teenage drug use, DWIs and public disturbances kept the small police force busy, but as his experience suggests, the death of someone at the hands of another was a rarity in this New York suburb.

Simmons had been alerted at home in the early morning hours of November 19 by Chief of Police Robert Baines, and was told to take charge of the investigation. Simmons had immediately left his home and driven over to Northern Westchester Hospital, where he was briefed on what was known by NCPD Sergeant Bruce Cathie.

In the treatment area of the hospital's ER, Simmons had had Carlos retell him and Officer Geraldez, briefly, the events of the evening leading up to the shootings. Simmons told the court that he'd found Carlos to be "lucid" and calm, despite having undergone the trauma of the altercation and having been shot. Simmons said he thought it was interesting that Carlos had guessed the gunman to be Colombian, since, according to Carlos, the man had never spoken.

Carlos had also told the detective that he'd defended some clients charged with drug violations, so he had a lot of enemies. Learning that the victim couple had a teenage daughter home alone, Simmons, despite Carlos' polite refusal, ordered a uniformed policeman to guard the home.

Before leaving the hospital, Simmons had taken possession of Peggy's clothes, made photos of the Montero and noted the blood, the interior contents and the bullet holes in the vehicle. He'd then had Sergeant Cathie, with assistance from the Mount Kisco PD, remove the SUV from the hospital ER lot and had it transported to the New Castle impound lot.

Before the sun rose that morning, Simmons had visited

the crime scene, where he too was surprised that no skid marks were evident, and then drove over to NCPD HQ to oversee the routine procedures of a felony investigation.

Later that morning Simmons had returned to the hospital, where, with Carlos' permission, he performed the gunshot primer swab, which, he explained to the jury, is a test for gunshot primer residue on a suspect's hand. The test results were negative for the right hand. Simmons didn't swab the left hand, as it was bandaged.

Carlos had also agreed to help a police sketch artist come up with a portrait of the gunman that could be distributed to other police departments and the press in hopes of identifying and apprehending him. This time Carlos described the gunman as "white, but not Irish-white." Again with the permission of Carlos, Detective Simmons had left the hospital with the clothes Carlos was wearing on Saturday night when he and his wife were shot.

The sketch artist had done his work on a seat beside Carlos' hospital bed. On a scale of one to ten in accuracy, Carlos gave it a nine.

On November 21, Simmons, along with fellow Detective Vargas, had witnessed the autopsy of Peggy Perez-Olivo and taken possession of the bullet removed from her brain by the county pathologist. That afternoon Simmons had driven over to the Perez-Olivo residence on Old House Lane, to which Carlos had been released, for yet another interview.

Simmons testified that Carlos had been "cooperative and was responsive," and readily agreed to give a DNA swab and expose his wound so the detective could photograph it. When he'd left the residence on Old House Lane, Simmons had written sixteen pages detailing the day the couple was shot. Simmons described Carlos' demeanor as "calm and subdued." The detective thought it curious that his tone had changed when he spoke of his source of income. Carlos had become evasive and offered up no information on the matter.

After the lunch break, Detective Simmons continued his testimony. He told the court how he'd retraced the steps and the route the Perez-Olivos had taken into Manhattan and back up to Westchester County the day of the shootings. He spoke of visiting the Chelsea Cinema on West 23rd Street, where the pair had watched *Volver*, a foreign film with Penélope Cruz. He also spent time reviewing the theater's security tapes of that day. Nothing suspicious had been found. The couple didn't appear to have been followed or watched. The detectives had visited the French restaurant and spoken with the maître d' and their waiter. Again, nothing suspicious had turned up.

The trip back to Chappaqua, using the route Carlos and Peggy had driven, raised more questions than it answered. The prosecution showed an aerial video to graphically make their point. Why did he take the out-of-the-way Taconic Parkway when the Saw Mill would have been more direct and quicker? Carlos said he'd been looking to gas up his near-empty Montero—yet, Simmons said, he could have taken the Saw Mill and gotten off by the convenient Pleasantville gas station. Instead he'd opted for the distant and out-of-the-way Millwood Exxon station at the intersection of Campfire Road and Route 100.

But there was another glaring question about his choices that night. Given the fact that he was going to the Millwood station, why hadn't he exited the Taconic at the Campfire Road exit, which was not even a quarter mile from the gas station? According to Carlos, he'd exited at Route 100/9A, far south of the Campfire Road turnoff, and driven the dark and quiet access road some five miles until being run off the road by the mysterious assailants at the spot a half-mile short of the Millwood Exxon station.

On November 29, Simmons, on another visit to the Perez-Olivo residence, had gotten the names of two disgruntled clients of Carlos who he believed might have been behind the shootings. Convicted murderer Elio Cruz had been paid a visit by Simmons at the upstate prison where he was incarcerated. Anthony Stevens, convicted of burglary and sentenced to 15 years in Sing Sing Prison, was also questioned. Both men had been cleared by Simmons as suspects.

When Carlos was confronted by Simmons about his long affair with Ileana Santana Poole, he owned up to it, but insisted that it had ended two years before. He told the detective his wife was unaware of the affair. It was at this time that Simmons learned of the accidental-death insurance policies on Peggy that totaled almost $900,000, with Carlos as the beneficiary.

Simmons believed he had put together a very strong circumstantial case against the husband of the deceased. The facts in the case were overwhelming. Carlos' excuse for being where they were when they'd been shot was a lame one. His account of the struggle and the shooting was unsubstantiated by the physical evidence. And how could his wife have slept through Carlos' struggle with the armed intruder? Plus, the defendant had a mistress. His license to practice law had been lifted, leaving him, by all appearances, broke and he was the beneficiary of his wife's insurance policies.

Mark Gazzola's testimony linking Carlos to the gun had to be in the back of jurors' minds as they heard Simmons' testimony. The defense had a formidable challenge, to prove their client's innocence. Their immediate task at hand was to chip away at Detective Simmons' findings, cumulatively the most damaging to their client. They got their shot at him on cross-examination that afternoon, the third day of testimony.

Chris McClure handled the cross-examination. The former ADA, who has a habit of wandering the courtroom while he speaks, immediately asked Simmons to confirm that this was only the second homicide investigation he had ever handled. Simmons confirmed that fact.

Portale also got the detective to reiterate that Carlos had been forthcoming and cooperative, and never asked to have a lawyer present. One detail the defense team was able to enter, and have confirmed by Simmons, was that Carlos often used the Exxon station in Millwood because it was cheaper and close to the health club he frequented just south of the station on Route 100.

Concerning his income, Carlos had told the detective

that he'd been involved in a business venture in Venezuela and that it was only when pressed for details that he begged off, saying, "Can we stay away from that?"

Also entered into the court record was Carlos' explanation that he hadn't taken the Saw Mill River Parkway because of the presence of traffic lights that the Taconic didn't have.

Defense Attorney Portale asked if it was a fact that, once the NCPD notified Carlos that he would be arrested and charged with the murder of his wife, his attorney Robert Buckley had requested that his client be picked up at his home. Simmons said it was and that the defendant quietly surrendered when the police arrived at Old House Lane with the warrant.

CHAPTER TWENTY-TWO:

A MOTIVE?

ANTHONY BRATTON, THE Deputy Chief Counsel for the New York Supreme Court, was called to the stand. Bratton testified that Carlos Perez-Olivo had been disbarred on August 3, 2006. The defense was successful before going to trial in preventing Bratton from relating what charges against the accused had been heard, and what reasons given, for his disbarment. The defense had successfully argued that such information was prejudicial to their client. As a result, Bratton was on the stand for less than five minutes.

The prosecution then called in succession two local bankers and two credit card investigators. The bankers referred to accounts maintained by the accused and recited account activities. Their testimony did not paint a rosy picture of the Perez-Olivo family's finances.

Tamara Hall, of JP Morgan Chase, in response to ADA Perrone's questions, recited the 2006 monthly balances of Carlos' checking account. The amounts fluctuated wildly, with a high of $65,732.97 in May to a low of $2.97 in November.

Luigi Tosto of Citibank told a similar story. He noted that at the time of the murder Carlos had $178.09 in his account.

Greg Tutelian, an investigator in the credit card services for the Bank of America, testified that the defendant had a balance of $9,528.19, and was over his credit limit. James Hughes of HSBC credit card services told the court that Mr. Perez-Olivo's two cards had been in collection in November 2006 for the amounts of $1,500 and $9,000.

On September 19, the fifth day of testimony, a parade of insurance investigators and account executives dutifully testified about what many court watchers opined was an unusually large number of accidental-death insurance policies.

As it turned out, the smallest policy was the only one that did not pay out. Rose Marie Hewig, an attorney for the New York State Retirement Association said they had refused to pay the $65,000 to sole beneficiary Carlos Perez-Olivo as long as he remained a suspect in his wife's death. The prosecution was also able to enter in the court record that Peggy's yearly salary was only $21,028. That was a number the jury would surely ponder while trying to justify the numerous insurance policies that were automatically debited from her Citibank checking account.

Insurance Examiner Lillian Cremin of The Hartford life insurance company testified that they had paid a total of $450,000 to the children of the decedent after Carlos waived his right to the money, since he was a suspect. Referring to the policy papers, Cremin said her company had been contacted within a month of Peggy's death, requesting payment on the five-year-old policy. Cremin also testified that the death benefit had been increased from $100,000 to $300,000 in September 2005 and another policy for $150,000 had been taken out at that time as well.

Regina Solomon of MetLife Insurance told a similar story. Her company had paid out $155,797.07 to the eldest son of the policy holder on February 29, 2008, after the primary beneficiary, her husband, waived his right to payment.

As he would do in all cross-examinations of the insurance witnesses, Attorney Portale got it on record that the policy premiums had been paid out of Peggy's checking account and that it was not unusual for claimants to request payment so soon after the death of the policy holder.

Michael Kalucki of the AIG insurance company testified that the $50,000 policy in the name of Peggy Perez-Olivo his company had written had lapsed after the one-year free trial period, but was reinstated after increasing its value to $100,000 one year before the murder.

Apparently Carlos had insured himself as well, but, according to Phoenix Life Insurance executive Thomas McCabe, Jr., the $500,000 policy listing Peggy as the beneficiary had lapsed for nonpayment just three months before the fatal incident on Route 100. ADA Perry Perrone made it clear by his questioning of the witness that Carlos had had a forty-five-day grace period to get the policy current, but he did not.

Later in the trial, a life insurance executive would testify about yet another policy on Peggy, and how Perez-Olivo attorney Robert Buckley had written on December 12 demanding payment.

CHAPTER TWENTY-THREE:

AN EXECUTION OR AN ERRANT SHOT?

OFFICER KELLY CLOSE of the NCPD is the accident reconstruction and auto expert for the department. He related how he'd disassembled the interior of the Montero and laid it bare in his search for any evidence that previous cursory searches had missed. He'd found nothing. His testimony suggested the prosecution's contention that there were only three shots fired from inside the vehicle: the one that was removed from Peggy's body, the bullet in the roof's lining and the one that had gone through the rear passenger's-side window and been lost. That would account for the three .32-caliber brass shell casings found, two in the car and one on the road shoulder.

Close's appearance in the witness box would dovetail with a ballistics expert the prosecution would later call who would testify that the bullet that exited the vehicle could not possibly be the one that had struck Carlos. The prosecution would contend that there had to have been a fourth shot fired outside the SUV, with Carlos discarding the casing as he did with the gun by tossing it in Echo Lake after he had superficially wounded himself.

Forensic scientist Brandi Benjamin would be the last witness of the week. Benjamin was with the Westchester County Forensic Division of Sciences. The crime lab was the province of the Westchester Department of Safety, better known as the County Police. The lab also did work for the smaller departments in the county that couldn't justify having their own. New Castle PD was one such department.

Benjamin's specialty was ballistics, but she would be

testifying on gunshot residue patterns analysis (GRPA), where the propellant residue on the contact material would be analyzed. Although Benjamin was no stranger to the witness box, this was only the third time she had been questioned as an expert on GRPA. That had defense attorney Richard Portale chomping at the bit to have a go at her when Benjamin was his witness to grill.

Benjamin, 32 years of age, was an eight-year veteran of the crime lab. Her unsmiling, succinct responses, conservative dress, straight unadorned hair and simple dark-framed glasses suggested a scientist more comfortable in a lab than testifying in open court. The prosecution was expecting her to be a formidable witness who would ice their case forensically.

Benjamin's GRPA findings regarding the bullet hole in the Montero's roof liner brought a quick objection from Portale. A heated exchange between counsels ensued over Benjamin's expertise in the field of GRPA. Judge Zambelli found it necessary to excuse the jury while it was hashed out.

Zambelli, clearly irked by Portale's persistence in challenging the witness's expertise, overruled his objections, but allowed for the jury to make their own determination on the matter when in deliberation.

Benjamin concluded from her analysis, dictated by lab protocol, that the gun's muzzle was ten to fourteen inches away from the liner, an unlikely scenario in the defendant's account of what had happened during the struggle for the gun.

After testifying that Carlos' superficial gunshot wound had appeared, from the residue analysis of his shirt, to be a contact wound, Benjamin tackled the GRPA on the front passenger headrest—the calling card of the bullet that had bisected Peggy's brain.

Over objections from the defense, the forensic scientist demonstrated, with the suspect handgun and the actual headrest from the Montero, how the fatal shot had most likely been fired. The telltale vaporous lead smudge on the bottom of the headrest indicated, she testified, a near-contact shooting of

The Perez-Olivo residence in Chappaqua, just down the street from the Clinton residence. *(Kevin F. McMurray)*

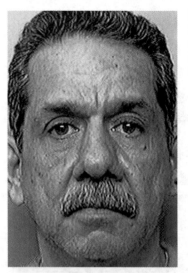

Mug shot of Carlos Perez-Olivo. *(Courtesy of Westchester County Department of Corrections)*

A photo of Peggy Perez-Olivo not long before her death in November 2006. *(Courtesy of the Perez-Olivo Family Collection)*

The scene of the crime. Note the patch of new asphalt where the original was taken as evidence for blood droppings. *(Kevin F. McMurray)*

Branches are cleared near the pond where the murder weapon was found. *(Kevin F. McMurray)*

The Walther PPK .32-caliber semi-automatic. Note the tang that protects the hand from slide bite. *(Kevin F. McMurray)*

Detective Anthony Tota, senior firearms examiner in the Ballistics Unit of the county lab. *(Kevin F. McMurray)*

Detective Artie Holzman, a ballistics expert with the Westchester County Crime Lab who retrieved the two spent bullets and three shell casings from the Perez-Olivos' Mitsubishi Montero. *(Kevin F. McMurray)*

Detective Tota shoots as Detective Holzman watches. *(Kevin F. McMurray)*

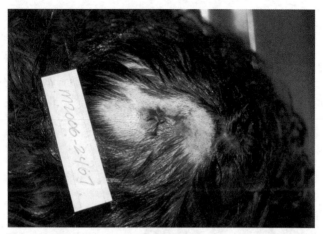

The autopsy photo of Peggy Perez-Olivo that was analyzed for stippling. *(Courtesy of Michael Archer)*

Private investigator for the defense, Danny Marrone. *(Kevin F. McMurray)*

LEFT TO RIGHT: Lt. Det. Marc Simmons, Det. Gary Beaumont, ADA Christine O'Connor, D.A. Janet DiFiore, ADA Perry Perrone, Det. Daniel Corrado, Det. Noel Vargas. The team that investigated and prosecuted Carlos Perez-Olivo. *(Kevin F. McMurray)*

Author Kevin F. McMurray and Carlos Perez-Olivo in a visiting room at Wende prison. *(Kevin F. McMurray)*

Carlos with Peggy, who's holding the young Carlitos, in Puerto Rico circa 1978. *(Courtesy of the Perez-Olivo Family Collection)*

the weapon. In other words, it was an execution-style type of shooting, where the muzzle of the gun had been inserted between the bottom of the headrest and the top of the backrest against Peggy's head—a space of two inches—and fired.

On Monday, September 22 Brandi Benjamin was back on the stand and finished up detailing her analysis of the headrest.

Robert Adamo, the next witness, was the supervisor of the county crime lab. The lab employs forty men and women, all of whom answer to Adamo, who has been there twenty-eight years. The senior forensic scientist was on the stand to present a video shot by the lab of a re-enactment of the struggle between the alleged gunman and Perez Olivo, as described by the defendant.

The effectiveness of the video was questionable, since it was amateurishly shot and clumsily acted out. To make matters worse, the withheld audio, which the defense insisted be heard, with the judge agreeing, was discordant, distracting and improper. Non-participants could be heard talking and laughing off camera. But the video, however poorly produced was, did depict just how preposterous Perez-Olivo's account of the fatal struggle for the gun. The jury's opinion of it could only be guessed at this point.

The very pregnant Susan Flaherty of the Westchester crime lab took the stand. Flaherty was the DNA expert assigned to the case. Bloodstains from the rear driver's-side door, back of the driver's seat, cargo area and steering wheel were found to have come from the defendant. Most important, DNA swabbings of the bullet recovered from the SUV's roof and the bullet hole in the rear driver's window came up negative for human tissue. That suggested that neither bullet had struck Carlos, lending credence to the prosecution's theory that a fourth shot had been fired outside the vehicle.

In their cross, defense attorney Richard Portale was able to get the forensic scientist for the county to admit that just because there was no DNA evidence belonging to their client on the recovered bullet or the bullet hole didn't mean that the bullets could not have struck Mr. Perez-Olivo first.

The last witness of the day was Dr. Michael Fischer, MD. He was the emergency room physician at Northern Westchester Hospital who'd treated Peggy Perez-Olivo on the evening of November 18.

Fischer testified that the patient had had no vital signs when she was wheeled into the ER. Standard techniques to revive her had failed. The middle-aged female, according to the trauma specialist, had "flatlined," but was revived when she was administered epinephrine, a drug that had, in effect, jump-started all of her vitals. She was then put on a ventilator. The treatment needed to keep her alive told the attending doctor that he was most likely dealing with a severe head injury. A close examination of her head, he told the court, had revealed a slight dimple or indentation in the center rear of her skull. He now knew he had a shooting victim, and the prognosis was not good. A neurosurgeon had been called down to confirm Fischer's diagnosis. Both men agreed that the woman had suffered a "life-ending injury" and there was nothing more that could be done. Peggy Perez-Olivo was brain-dead. Dr. Fischer's only other duty after notifying next of kin had been to assist in any harvesting of organs for donation.

Fischer said the bullet hole, from experience, appeared to be an "execution-style wound." That observation was allowed by Judge Zambelli on objection from the defense only as an opinion of a trauma physician and not an expert pronouncement of a trained ballistic pathologist.

On the seventh day of testimony the county lab's gunshot primer residue expert, Ron Prip, was the first to take the stand. Primer residue is usually found on anything within several feet of the muzzle of the fired handgun—the closer to the muzzle, the higher the count of primer residue. The highest count he'd found was on Carlos' white polo shirt cuff.

Anti-fraud investigator Craig Bruno represented the car

insurance company responsible for Peggy's no-fault life insurance policy. Bruno gave what would later prove to be crucial testimony. Asked to characterize his relationship with his wife, Carlos had replied that she was "the love of his life." The investigator then asked, with apologies, if he'd killed his wife. Carlos said that he had not, but that he'd received threats due to the nature of his law practice.

Bruno had questioned Carlos in detail about the evening the couple was shot. Carlos told the investigator the details of the couple's evening in the city and answered questions about how they'd been run off the road in Millwood, where he had gone to gas up. Carlos said they'd been going no faster than 35 miles per hour—which would explain the absence of skid marks or signs of a collision. He described the car with the three men and how one of them had jumped into the back seat of the Montero. Carlos said he had lost his temper, unsnapped his seat belt and gotten into a tussle with the "Hispanic" gunman, who never spoke a word. Bruno got Carlos' blow-by-blow account of the struggle with the armed intruder and how Peggy had never awakened from her slumber.

Carlos talked about how the gun had fired two to four times during the struggle. He said he was no gun expert and couldn't say what kind of handgun it was. ADA Perrone asked Bruno to describe Carlos' demeanor during the interview. He said Carlos had been "calm and detached." It was a description that would come back to haunt the defense.

Steven Kohler, the Westchester crime lab fingerprint expert, testified how no useable latent prints had been found on the gun or the shell casings. Robert Barber, another crime-scene fingerprint expert for the county lab, testified that the only useable latent print had been found on the driver's-side rear door. It was a thumbprint belonging to Carlos.

Dr. Miller Hyland presented the autopsy for the prosecution. Hyland is the chief medical examiner for Westchester County. He had been at that post for twenty-five years and oversaw a staff of 115 employees; however, from the doctor's testimony, there appeared to be a problem at the

department's pathologist level. Dr. Lewis Rho had left the
M.E.'s office and did not testify about his autopsy of Peggy
Perez-Olivo at the trial. Dr. Duc Duong, assisting pathologist on the procedure, was now employed in California and
was never contacted about testifying. That left the chief
M.E. no choice but to present the autopsy as evidence himself, even though he had not been present when Peggy was
autopsied.

Dr. Hyland seemed tired and bored during his testimony, and he was clearly aggravated, sounding like a busy
executive having to waste time with the trivial departmental
minutiae.

The M.E. agreed with the findings of Dr. Rho, namely
that Peggy Perez-Olivo had died from a single gunshot
wound to the head, with the bullet bisecting the brain from
back to front, coming to rest near the frontal bone area of
the brain. Dr. Hyland demonstrated with the gun and a Styrofoam dummy head how the victim had been shot, and
that the "stippling"—gunshot residue and powder burns—
clearly visible around the wound proved it. He further explained, indicating on a blown-up version of the photo on a
TV screen set up for the jury, that the tight dense pattern of
the stippling indicated that the victim had been dispatched
with an execution-like shot.

In his cross, defense attorney McClure cited the issue of
the missing pathologists. He was also successful in getting
Dr. Hyland to reluctantly admit that his agreement with
Rho's conclusions was based solely on autopsy photographs,
he having never set foot in the autopsy room when the procedure was conducted.

There was also one issue of particular interest: the "stippling" around the entrance wound in the back of the murdered woman's head. McClure indicated that the defense
would pursue it when they called their own expert witness.

If the defense was going to challenge the prosecution's contention that Peggy had been executed, they would also have

to discredit the next witness, Susan Tezzie. Tezzie was a forensic chemist with the county lab who specialized in chemical analysis of gunshot residue (GSR). She said under oath that the vaporous lead she found on the victim's headrest indicated that the muzzle of the murder weapon either had to be touching or flush with the headrest.

Her testimony regarding the bullet in the roof liner and the bullet hole in the window indicated that the liner bullet had been fired from at least fourteen inches away at an angle, and the bullet that struck the car window had most likely been fired at a 90-degree angle. The testimony seemed to counter the defense's contention of how and where the bullets had been fired. The question about the bullet that the defense intimated had hit the contorted Carlos and exited the window at a 90-degree angle was left begging for an answer. Tezzie stuck to her conclusions under cross-examination from defense attorney Portale.

To show the jury that the Perez-Olivo Montero was properly handled as evidence, Detective Noel Vargas of the NCPD explained in detail the careful transporting of it from the Chappaqua impound lot to the county lab in White Plains.

The last witness of the day was Detective Anthony Tota. Tota is the senior firearms examiner in the Ballistics Unit of the county lab and has thirty-eight years of experience with the New York Police Department and the county. From the two recovered bullets—the roof liner, and the victim—he concluded that they could come from only one gun: the .32-caliber Walther PPK recovered from Echo Lake that he was now holding in his hands.

When Tota stepped down from the witness box, the People, ADA Perrone said, rested their case. They had called forty-three witnesses across eight days of testimony. The trial was going faster than anyone had anticipated.

CHAPTER TWENTY-FOUR:

CALLING FOR THE DEFENSE . . .

ON FRIDAY, SEPTEMBER 26, the defense finally got their opportunity to present witnesses. First in line was Alysia Perez-Hall, the youngest child of Peggy and Carlos Perez-Olivo. Prior to calling the 19-year-old daughter, the defense wanted the court to reconsider hearing a witness who had just come to their attention. They claimed the witness had experienced a similar episode of violence on Route 100 around the time Peggy was shot and killed. He too had been run off the road by a mystery vehicle, but had escaped. Despite Portale's impassioned plea, Judge Zambelli ruled in the prosecution's favor by not allowing the man to testify, since there was an "insufficient link" to bring him to the stand so late in the trial.

Alysia Perez-Olivo, dressed in black slacks and blouse with a grey jacket, smiled nervously at her dad at the defense table. She took the witness stand after saying "I do" to the oath, administered by Judge Zambelli.

In a little-girl voice, often punctuated by an endearing giggle, she told the court of her present status as an undergraduate art student at a Maryland college. At the prompting of attorney McClure, she told the jury of a happy family life, even though they'd moved around a lot, and sometimes money had been tight. She spoke of the close relationship she'd had with her parents, especially her mom, who was her "best friend." Her parents, she cheerfully related, had been devoted to one another and were still very much in love. Alysia said her dad would often stop her mom in her tracks just to hug and kiss her, and that they often held hands. "They did everything together," she said. There was no way her dad would ever hurt her mom.

The jury was visibly charmed by the cute, effervescent young girl, leaning forward to hear her every word. It was obvious that the defense had started off with a home run, but the question on the minds of all the courtroom watchers was, Could the defense hit some more and chip away at the strong circumstantial case the prosecution had built?

The defense's second witness was a gun expert whose credentials as a gunsmith and collector were reluctantly acceptable to the prosecution.

Louis Romero owned and operated a gun store in Yonkers, the county's largest and southernmost community, which abutted the Bronx. He said he was very familiar with the .32-caliber Walther PPK that was handed him to inspect.

McClure asked Romero if the gun was rare and valuable to a collector. "Not to me," he said. When asked why that was, the short stocky gun expert said that the Walther's slide and main frame serial numbers didn't match, making it virtually worthless to a serious collector. Romero also testified that the gun, even a prewar model, wasn't all that rare, since the Germans made hundreds of thousands of them, and the model he was holding—the murder weapon—could easily be bought through a dealer or on the Internet.

The defense, with this expert witness, was attacking the expertise of the people's star witness, Mark Gazzola, whose testimony had placed the murder weapon in Carlos' hand. As Romero stepped down, court watchers were left wondering if the defense had planted the seed of doubt in any of the jurors' minds.

That question would be answered sooner than anyone had thought.

CHAPTER TWENTY-FIVE:

A REASONABLE DOUBT

ON AN AUGUST evening in 2005, Bob Wright and his wife Trish were traveling north on Route 9A, heading back home to Katonah after dinner at a restaurant and a late movie at the multiplex in nearby Hawthorne. It was after midnight and the couple were looking forward to calling it a day and climbing into bed.

Bob, a slight, boyish-looking 40-year-old, remarked to his wife how dark and deserted the road was. Bob, among other professional pursuits, was an accountant, and a detail man by nature. The eerie darkness made him think of an earlier conversation the couple had had about traveling together, and what would become of their two kids if something happened to him and his wife. They had resolved not to make that mistake in the future and, when possible, travel separately. Of course, tonight an exception could be made, since they hadn't driven more than twenty miles away from their house.

Minutes later, where Route 9A became Route 100, Bob noticed a darkened parked car off on the right shoulder as he sped by. He wondered if it was a deserted automobile or a disabled one. If it were disabled, Bob grumbled to himself, they should have had their emergency lights on. Moments later, looking into his rear-view mirror, a dark shadow filled the frame. Suddenly the darkness exploded into a crescendo of light. Squinting into his rear-view, he could barely see. The vehicle, with its brights now piercing the darkness, had snuck up on him with lights off, then quickly fallen into their draft a couple of feet back, before flicking them on. If the mystery car's goal was to "scare the shit out of us," Bob said, "it succeeded."

Staring away from the blinding light, he instinctively gunned the engine of his sleek Mercedes 500SL. The pursuing car kept pace, close enough to hitch itself to Bob's bumper.

Bob was cursing the "bastard," while Trish tightened her grip on her seat. She had been having a recurring dream that started just like this, and ended in gunfire. Without thinking, she slid down low in her seat so her head was below the dashboard and wasn't a target.

Bob had no intention of letting the pursuing car overtake them, knowing that it would then be in a position to run them off the road. He stamped the accelerator pedal of the expensive roadster to the floor. The mystery car fell off the pace when the high-horsepowered Mercedes hit 100 miles per hour, but it showed no signs of breaking off the chase. After what seemed like an eternity to the couple, the lights of the Millwood gas station appeared up ahead. Bob didn't ease up on the gas. Suddenly the mystery vehicle broke off the chase and made a sharp left and sped up Route 133.

Breathing a sigh of relief, Bob watched in his rear-view as the taillights of their pursuer were swallowed up by the darkness.

Pulling into the Mobil gas station on the corner of Campfire Road and Poole 100, Bob was heartened by the presence of a New Castle police patrol car. Bob popped out of his Mercedes and walked up to the idling black-and-white.

Still on an adrenaline high, he told the cop in a nervous clip what had just happened to him and his wife just seconds ago. Hearing him out, the officer told him to step back as he slipped his cruiser into drive and raced off in the direction of Route 133. Bob never gave him his name or address. The Wrights dutifully waited around for several minutes to see if the cop would return, and when he didn't, they went home to bed. Bob figured police would somehow get in touch with him to get the details so an investigation could be launched. They never did.

On the morning of November 19, 2006, Bob Wright listened incredulously to the news report on the local Westchester TV station about the details of the shooting death of Peggy Perez-Olivo on Route 100 in Millwood. Bob immediately picked up his phone and dialed 411 for the New Castle Police Department's phone number. It was déjà-vu time for Bob Wright.

Telling the officer who answered what he was calling about, Bob was switched over to another line, where a detective would take his statement. Bob told the detective of his and his wife's close encounter on that same stretch of road fifteen months before. The cop dutifully took down all the details of the incident and asked a few questions, then told Bob he would be contacted by a detective later. Detective Daniel Corrado did call later that day and had Bob retell his story, asking a few questions about the details. Satisfied that he had done his civic duty, Bob forgot about the matter until he was once again traveling through Millwood on Route 100.

In the approximate area where his incident had taken place, there was a roadblock manned by cops who were stopping all vehicles traveling in both directions and talking to the drivers. Bob thought it was a car registration or inspection check. He was surprised to learn it was about the shooting death of the Chappaqua woman two weeks before.

Bob told the officer he had already given a statement to the cops, but would be happy to give another. One of the plainclothesmen at the stop remembered Bob and told him that they would be contacting him soon. It would be two years before he would hear something from the authorities again concerning his experience on Route 100. It was not, however, the police or the DA's office that came calling this time. It was defense Private Investigator Danny Marrone.

When Marrone pulled into the long driveway that snaked up to the large yellow house on the hill, he remembers thinking, "Finally, a credible witness."

By all appearances, he was right. Bob was an accountant and the owner of a couple of businesses that were pretty successful, from the look of things. The huge new house he was about to enter had to have cost well in excess of $1 million. The neighbors' homes were equally impressive.

Bob was a "tightly wound" type of guy, something his slight, wiry frame attested to. Marrone knew guys like Bob Wright didn't have the slowed-down metabolism needed to put on weight. The fact that it had taken five calls to convince him to submit to an interview by the private investigator also spoke volumes about his personality.

The former NYPD detective found Bob's story to be believable, and it was backed up by his wife, who was a playful foil to her husband's nervousness. Wright didn't seem like a guy hungry for his fifteen minutes of celebrity. On the contrary, he shunned publicity and was worried about being found out by the media and becoming a target for the cameras and microphones—a nightmarish prospect for him.

Marrone had obtained what McClure and Portale had hoped for: a witness who would give credence to Carlos' story of being run off the road by a mysterious car. Bob was notified by McClure to be in court on Friday, September 19, and be ready to testify.

As Wright nervously paced the hallway outside Courtroom 203, McClure argued for his testimony to be heard. It was to no avail. Judge Zambelli denied the defense's request to seat Wright in the witness box. "A pissed-off Portale" came out and told Wright he would not be testifying after all. Wright happily left the building.

On his way to his parked car, Wright took five phone calls from the New Castle Police Department. On each call, a detective on the other end of the line wanted to know who he was and what he was going to testify to. Wright deferred all questions to his lawyer. He ignored the last two calls.

On his way home, pondering his brush with the legal system, he worried about how justice was dispensed. He was troubled that an innocent man might be about to be rail-roaded into prison for life.

McClure's recollection of the issue is that Judge Zambelli believed that it was too attenuated because the witness couldn't say that the color of the car was green or that it was driven by male Hispanics.

"Additionally," McClure said, "I believe her quote was 'That could have happened anywhere in the county.' Despite the fact it was the same stretch of road, the same night of the week, and the same time of night."

CHAPTER TWENTY-SIX:

MERCED

THE SECOND OLDEST son of Carlos and Peggy became the third witness for the defense.

Merced Perez-Hall, 25, lived in Colorado, where he was attending graduate school. McClure asked him to explain his surname, why it was different from his parents'. Merced told the jury that it was a Latino tradition to incorporate your mother's maiden name with your father's, out of respect to your roots. All three siblings had complied with it.

Merced spoke of how he'd been awakened by a ringing phone in the early morning hours of November 18, and told by his brother Carlitos' wife that his parents had been in an "accident." Merced rushed home to Chappaqua and made it to the hospital the next morning, only to learn that his mother had been shot dead. He claimed that he had never seen his father in such a hysterical state, crying over and over that it was "all his fault." Merced opted not to see his mother's remains, telling the court that he wanted to remember her as she was the last time he had seen her: alive, and her usual buoyant self.

Merced, at the urging of attorney McClure, described his dad in the weeks that followed his mother's death as a "zombie," moping about their home on Old House Lane. His dad was no longer the happy, outgoing, responsible and fun-loving guy he had been. Carlitos had taken charge of all the family business, since their dad was "useless," due to the depression brought on by the death of his wife.

Merced attested to his parents' loving relationship and how he had "a great relationship with both of them." Echoing

Alysia's sentiments, he said his father had treated his mother exceptionally well and that he would never have harmed her. The middle child related that his friends often said how lucky he was to have the "perfect family life."

Regarding his father's disbarment and his extramarital affair, Merced said it was all news to him. He said he only learned of it after the incident from one of the news reporters who'd swooped down on them in the wake of the murder.

As for the Walther PPK, Merced claimed he'd never seen his father handle a firearm, no less own one, as he "hated guns." The ADAs declined to cross-examine the witness.

The next witnesses were two of Peggy's five sisters. Theresa Koch is a former nun and now a mother to ten grown children, who lives in the blue-grass horse country of Kentucky. Laura Labowsky, a mother to five kids, traveled up from Texas to testify, like her sister Theresa, on behalf of their brother-in-law Carlos. The two middle-aged women told of a couple devoted to each other and how they were the life of the party at all the family get-togethers. Theresa and Laura also spoke of how visibly "devastated" Carlos had been over Peggy's death and how they couldn't imagine Carlos doing any harm to their sister.

Both women were asked in cross to explain the absence of their sister Joanne, by all accounts the sibling closest to the deceased. They could not.

Carlos and Peggy's eldest son and namesake would be the last to take the stand that day, and perhaps the most anticipated of the defense's witnesses. Tall, thin and handsome, and dressed impeccably in a dark conservative pinstriped suit, it was not hard to imagine "Carlitos" as the spitting image of his father twenty-five years before. Carlitos, smiling broadly, took the oath and identified himself in a clear baritone. The 30-year-old, like his dad, was an attorney. Unlike his dad, he had forgone criminal law in lieu of the more sedate and less stressful real estate law. Carlitos practiced in New York City and resided with his wife in Brooklyn. The prosecution had saved all the hard questions for the new head of the family.

Carlitos said he hoped to emulate his parents in his married life, since theirs was "perfect." He called his dad a "great pal," who was generous with his time and money. Like his brother and sister, Carlitos' college and law school tuition had been paid by his father. Although not a social obligation, Carlos had paid for part of his son's wedding, even after footing the bill for a huge rehearsal dinner. Carlos also gave his son and daughter-in-law $3,000 for their honeymoon. Carlitos told the jury that his father had bought cars for all the kids and his wife. It was a boom-and-bust lifestyle for the family, but his dad always had a handle on it.

When Carlitos had arrived at the hospital Sunday morning, he'd thought his dad had gotten drunk and wrecked the car. When he found his father and learned that his mother had been shot and killed, he "lost it." He and his dad hugged each other and cried. His dad, over and over again, kept blaming himself for his wife's death.

Carlitos choked up on the stand when recounting the scene at the hospital. He closed his eyes tight to stem the flow of tears, straightened his jacket and after a few moments of dead silence in the courtroom, he nodded to Chris McClure that he was ready to continue. Judge Zambelli asked him if he wanted to take ten minutes to compose himself. Carlitos respectfully declined.

Carlos' namesake testified that his dad was a "destroyed man," and that their home on Old House Lane had been reduced to a "tomb," with his father totally unfit to take care of himself, no less the family and home. Carlitos handled the funeral arrangements for his mother. He and attorney friend Robert Buckley had also seen to it that the insurance companies were notified and that the funds-collection process was started. Carlitos confessed that he'd been surprised at the big dollar amounts of his mom's policies.

In the cross, Perry Perrone threw Carlitos a curve after setting him up with some softballs. Carlitos was caught off-guard.

"Isn't it true," the ADA deftly asked while shuffling some papers on the defense table, "that you once said you could never practice with your father because he worked too close to the line [of legality]?" There was a spark of anger in Carlitos' eyes, but the sustained objections from the defense table silenced him. He would not have to explain himself. Although the jury was told to ignore the exchange, it had to make them wonder why the son, who claimed to love and admire his father, did not pursue criminal law and practice with his dad. Perrone asked what had been done with his mom's clothes and personal items. His father, he admitted, told him to "get rid of [them]" because they were a daily reminder of his wife's absence. So the family had held a tag sale in the front yard of their home.

CHAPTER TWENTY-SEVEN:

DUELING PATHOLOGISTS

AFTER THE WEEKEND break, on Monday morning, Perez-Olivo friend and attorney Robert Buckley made an abbreviated visit to the stand. Buckley was considerably older than his former law school classmate Carlitos, more a contemporary of the defendant. He confirmed that he had been asked to help in dealing with the insurance claims and that the work was strictly procedural.

In cross-examination the prosecution tried to delve slyly into the matter of disbarment. The tactic was vociferously objected to by the defense. Zambelli sustained their objections, no doubt because the lines of questioning trod dangerously close to the verboten subject of the cause for disbarment. Perrone had no further questions. Richard Portale asked that Dr. Thomas Andrew be called to the stand.

Dr. Andrew is a board-certified anatomical pathologist and presently the chief medical examiner of New Hampshire. Although the small New England state averaged just twenty homicides a year, Dr. Andrew estimated that during the length of his career, which had mostly been spent in New York City, he performed over 4,000 autopsies, of which at least 700 were victims of gunshot wounds. He also rattled off his educational background, his degrees, specialties, affiliations and published works. Dr. Andrew knew the routine, and was obviously an old hand at testifying in homicide cases for defendants who could afford him. Without even being asked, he volunteered the fee he charges for his research, time spent on travel and testimony. He'd received a $5,600 retainer from Perez-Olivo's attorneys, plus

$350 an hour. From his testimony, he appeared to be worth it.

Portale asked him if he had reviewed the autopsy of Peggy Perez-Olivo. He responded that he had.

Although agreeing with the county's autopsy report, Dr. Andrew disagreed with the pathologist's finding of stippling around the bullet entrance wound. He'd examined the autopsy photos and concluded that it was not gunshot residue, but simply hair follicles, some of them inflamed. The supposed stippling effect, Dr. Andrew said, was a result of the ER nurses shaving the area of the wound so that it could be bandaged properly.

Also, there were no other signs of an execution-type shot, specifically no gun soot around the wound, which he said he would have expected. Dr. Andrew, however, did concede that a thick head of hair could have prevented any significant GSR. It also could have been washed away with hydrogen peroxide, a wound-cleaning agent, when medical professionals tried to save Peggy's life.

The testifying pathologist concluded that it was not a contact or near-contact wound, but a bullet fired from six to fourteen inches away from the head of the victim.

In their cross, the prosecution took the defense witness to task over a couple of issues. A quiet medical examiner's office in New Hampshire was one of those issues. The implication was that twenty homicides a year was hardly enough to qualify one as an expert in ballistics and gunshot pattern analysis. Proud of his state's low homicide total, the New Hampshire medical examiner reminded ADA Perrone of his service in New York City, the busiest medical examiner's office in the world.

He was also asked to address the scandal involving two of the deputies in his small department who had stolen property from the dead and had illegal dealings with private funeral homes. Without spelling it out for the jury, the prosecution subtly questioned his competence as a manager in his public service position. While the pair of state employees had started their illegal activities before Andrews' arrival, it did, he admitted, continue under his watch.

CHAPTER TWENTY-EIGHT:

HISTORY REPEATED

UNLIKE THE PROSECUTION, the defense saved their best witness for last. In this case, the closing defense "witness" was an audiotape of the dramatic 911 call that Carlos had made after the shooting. The call lasted 12½ minutes. If Carlos was guilty, he deserved an Academy Award for the performance.

Alysia and Merced Perez-Hall left the courtroom while Carlitos stayed to hear the tape. The jury was provided transcripts, and they followed as it played to the courtroom.

The audiotape started with a call from a motorist alerting the police of a drunk driver on the Taconic Parkway. After hanging up from that call, the officer picked up the next call before the second ring.

Carlos was heard sucking hard for his breath as the dispatcher was trying to determine where he was . . .

911 Operator: Hello, nine-one-one.

Carlos: Hi [gasping] I just got m . . . I just . . . [gasping]

911 Operator: Are you in Ossining?

Carlos: [gasp]

911 Operator: Are you in Ossining?

Carlos: [gasp] I just got shot. . . .

911 Operator: Okay. Are you in Ossining?

Carlos: [gasp]

911 Operator: I'm los . . . Are you in Ossining?

Carlos: I'm on my way. [gasp] I'm trying to get to
Northern Westchester . . .

911 Operator: You're trying to get to Northern
Westchester? Are you in the city of Ossining though?

Carlos: [gasping] I . . .

Police Officer: This is town of Ossining Police. Is this
a call from a residence?

911 Operator: No, no, no, sorry, it isn't . . . No, no
[speaking at same time]

Carlos: [gasp] We got st . . . [gasp] We got stopped in
the car . . . [gasp] We got stopped at the side of the
road . . .

911 Operator: Okay.

Carlos: I'm going on 133 [gasping].

Carlos: [gasping] I'm trying to get . . . I'm driving . . .
I'm trying to to get to Northern Westchester . . .

Police Officer: Okay, okay. . . . Okay. Where was . . .

911 Operator: Okay, okay, you got . . .

Carlos: [gasping] I think my wife . . . I think my wife
is . . .

Police Officer: Okay

Carlos: My wife got shot . . .

Police Officer: Okay

911 Operator: All right. Listen, I'm here. I'm on the phone. How about you both come into Ossining? Are you on the highway?

Carlos: I'm on 133. I'm trying to g . . .

Police Officer: How close to Ossining are you? Do you know where you are on 133? What do you see out your window?

Carlos: [gasping] I just passed 120 and 133. . . . I've got . . . I've got to go to Northern Westchester . . . It was a guy . . . It was a guy . . . It was . . . It was a guy with blue jeans . . . [gasp]

Police Officer: Okay, what happened to you?

Carlos: Blue jeans, blue jeans . . .

Police Officer: What happened . . . What happened to you?

Carlos: He ran me off the road . . .

Police Officer: He ran you off the road?

Carlos: Yeah . . . On the back . . . on the back seat and . . .

Police Officer: Okay. Are you driving . . . are you driving a car right now?

Carlos: [gasping and voice rising] That's why I'm taking . . . I'm taking my wife to the . . . [voice hysterical] I'm telling you, I'm going to the hospital . . . I think she may be . . . I think . . . [very heavy gasping]

Police Officer: Okay . . . Where?

Carlos: She got shot . . . [cry and voice rising again]

911 Operator: Okay, okay.

Police Officer: Okay. Take it easy. She got shot, you say?

Carlos: Yes! . . . ?? I mean, I tried to fight the guy . . . I was stupid . . . I . . .

911 Operator: Okay. We can get . . . We can get an ambulance . . .

Police Officer: I've got to get an ambulance to you . . . wherever you are on 133 . . .

Carlos: I'm driving, I'm driving, I'm getting there, I'm going to get there . . . .

As the recording proceeded, Carlitos got up from his first-row seat and bolted for the door in tears.

The jury kept its cool. No emotion passed any face. Other than intently listening to the emergency call, they appeared unmoved by what they were hearing. It was if they had heard this kind of dramatic audio a thousand times before.

911 Operator: Are you on the Taconic State Parkway?

Police Officer: Where?

Carlos: I'm on 133, I'm going towards Mount Kisco . . .
I'm towards Northern Westchester . . . But you just try
get a police car and find the guy . . . blue jeans . . .

911 Operator: Okay, all right, so you're at 133—

Carlos: Late . . . late . . . late . . . late vehicle . . . car . . .
late veh . . .

Police Officer: All right, listen. Are you on 133
heading towards 100?

Carlos: Yeah . . . I ju . . . I just passed . . . I just passed
Seven Bridges . . . Seven Bridges . . . I just passed Seven
Bridges . . .

Police Officer: All right Seven Bridges road on 133?

Carlos: Yes, yes. I'm on my way . . . I love her . . .

Police Officer: Look, I need you to come in . . .

[gasping, stuttering, inaudible]

Police Officer: I don't want you to get into an accident.
I need you to stop somewhere where the police can get
you . . .

Carlos: I can't stop. . . . I can't stop. . . . I've got to get
my wife to the hospital. . . . I can't stop. . . . I can't
stop. . . . I'm . . . I'm all right. . . . I'll get there. . . .
Don't worry. . . . Just . . . just . . . try . . . try and get a
patrol car and see if you can get this guy . . . Please,
please, please . . .

Police Officer: Okay. What . . . What . . . What kind of
car is it?

Carlos: He . . . He . . . He had like a . . . He . . .
The guy had a . . . a . . . a . . . blue like a . . . late model
Toyota . . . a . . . a . . . a . . . Hispanic Guy . . . H . . .
H . . . H . . . H . . . Hispanic Guy . . .

Police Officer: Did you get a license plate number?
[Stuttering over talking police officer inaudible]

Carlos: Hell, no . . . . No.

Police Officer: Where did this . . . Where did this
shooting take place?

Carlos: [gasping] He put me off the road . . . I was . . . I
was still . . . Trying . . . trying to get gasoline . . .

Police Officer: What . . . This happened . . . this
happened at a gas station?

Carlos: No, no, . . . I was going to the gas station . . . I
was . . . I was going to the gas station . . . I was . . . I
was . . . I was going to the gas station . . . be . . . be . . .
before the Taconic?

Police Officer: What . . . What gas station was it? Do
you remember?

Carlos: I don't . . . I don't know. . . . I don't . . . Oh, ow,
shit . . . Fuck!

Police Officer: Where . . . Where are you now?

Carlos: I don't know. . . . I'm going toward Mount
Kisco. . . . I'm going toward Mount Kisco. . . . I'm . . .

Police Officer: Are you going to Northern Westchester
Hospital in Mount Kisco?

Carlos: Yes. . . . Yes. . . . Yes. . . . Yes. . . . Yes. . . .

Police Officer: All right.

Carlos: If I make it . . . If I make it . . . I'm going to try and make it . . . I'm going to try and make it . . .

Police Officer: What . . . What . . . What road are you on now?

Carlos: Oh Shit. . . . 130 . . . 130 . . . 133, I just passed . . . I just passed the Presb . . . I just passed . . . I just passed the Presbyterian . . . Oh, shit. . . . Presbyterian . . . Shit . . . Presbyterian ch . . . Presbyterian church . . .

Police Officer: The Presbyterian church?

Carlos: [groaning] Yeah. . . . Yeah. . . . Yeah.

911 Operator: What kind of car are you driving?

Police Officer: What are you . . . What are you driving?

Carlos: I'm in a . . . I'm in a . . . I'm in a Mit . . . in a—[breaks off with groans]

Police Officer: Are you injured . . . Are you injured too?

Carlos: Yeah. . . . Yeah. . . . Shot. . . . Yes . . . Yes . . . Yes, I'm shot. . . . I'm fine, fine. . . . I'm . . . I'm . . . I'm shot on the side . . . and I'm fine. . . .

Police Officer: [overtalking, almost inaudible] Sir, I believe . . .

Carlos: I got shot also, see. I'm going to need some . . . some medical attention. Please put a . . . put a hold now, please. . . . [inaudible] . . . You've got to get to the son-of-a-bitch. . . .

Police Officer: Listen to me. Listen to me [overtalking—inaudible] I've got to take care of you first . . . both of you.

Carlos [loud]: Forget about me. . . . My wife . . . My wife is important, not [voice pitch escalating] me. . . . Not me. . . . Not me. . . . Not me. . . . [Voice fading]

Police Officer: Yes, but listen, I don't want you crashing.

Carlos: Well, I'm not crashing . . .

Police Officer: I want to help.

Carlos: [gasping] I'm not . . . I'm just . . . I'm just . . . I'm . . . I'm just . . . I'm just . . . [Heavy panting and gasping]

911 Operator: Where are you driving down 133?

Police Officer: Where on 133 are you now?

Carlos: I'm about . . . I'm about . . . [Voice hysterical and high-pitched—inaudible] God damn it! [cries and groans] . . .

Police Officer: Where . . . Where are . . . Where are you now?

Carlos: I'm . . . [Cries and shouts—inaudible] [Overtalking, all parties—inaudible]

Police Officer: I need you to pull over.

911 Operator: You have to pull over. . . .
(Overtalking—inaudible)

Police Officer: Sir, I . . .

Carlos: [high-pitched and crying] I'm not pulling
over. . . . I'm not pulling over. . . . I'm not pulling
over. . . . I'm not . . . I'm not . . . I'm not pulling
over. . . . I'm not . . . I'm not pulling over. . . .
[Gibberish, cries, repetition]

Police Officer: Where are you now?

Carlos: [High-pitched cries, unable to identify words] I
don't know . . . [High-pitched speech] . . . I'm almost
there.

911 Operator: We can get the ambulance to you faster
than you driving; you might get into another accident.

Police Officer: Sir, I need to know where you are
before . . . if you pass out and don't make it.

Carlos: [High-pitched cries, unidentifiable words] . . .
Got to get . . . Got to get my wife . . .

911 Operator: Pull over right now. Pull over.

Police Officer: I need you to pull over. I need to get the
emergency medics to you to get to the hospital. Where
are you now?

Carlos: [Unidentified words] . . . I'm almost there . . .
I'm almost there . . . I'm almost there . . . I'm almost
there . . . I'm almost there . . . I'm al . . . [Breaks off
with cry]

911 Operator: What kind of car are you in, sir?

Police Officer: What road are you on now?

Carlos: I'm . . . I'm . . . I'm almost in Mount . . . I'm almost in Mount Kis . . . I'm almost in . . . Ow! Sh . . . I'm almost in Mount Kisco. . . . I'm almost in Mount . . .

911 Operator: You're almost in Mount Kisco now? You're still on 133?

Carlos: [cries—inaudible]

Police Officer: What kind of car are you driving?

Police Officer: Hello?

Police Officer: Hello?

911 Operator: I think his phone went out. . . . I think he's still there though. . . . The line . . .

Police Officer: Hello?

911 Operator: Oh no, the line's not there, he dropped it.

CHAPTER TWENTY-NINE:

THE END IN SIGHT

AFTER A TWO-DAY break while the court waited for the next and last witness to recover from an illness, the gallery filled up with media, kin and the curious—all in anticipation of a verdict, since the word had it that the trial would be going to the jury for a decision.

Dr. Albert Harper was the defense's ballistics expert. Harper's résumé certainly was impressive. Besides a slew of degrees in everything from forensic anthropology to law, Dr. Harper had also taught forensic courses for over eighteen years and had been published often. He is presently the director of the prestigious Henry C. Lee Institute of Forensic Science at the University of New Haven and a consultant to the Connecticut Office of the Chief Medical Examiner.

Dr. Harper had been given access to all the physical evidence in the case, from the murder weapon to the SUV, and, with his angle measurer and dowels, came up with conclusions the defense was eager to have the jury hear.

He disagreed with the prosecution's expert's conclusion that the bullet hole in the window had been fired at a 90-degree angle to the window. Andrews said it had been from a lesser angle, probably 70 degrees, which made the defense's contention that Carlos had been shot inside the car more plausible. Showing the photos of the dowels protruding from the bullet hole, Andrew also pointed out that Detective Tota, the county forensics officer, had failed to take into consideration the angle of the window from the floor of the car. Like most car windows, the Montero's don't go up and down on a straight 90-degree angle—there is a slight bow to it, which would affect the bullet trajectory.

Dr. Harper employed a Styrofoam dummy and found that when he placed it in what looked like a painfully contorted prone position he could prove with a dowel how, when the gun fired, it could have struck Carlos and exited the vehicle through the window.

The testimony of the defense ballistics expert was picked up again on Monday morning. There were sidebars among counsel and Judge Zambelli about points made by Dr. Harper centering on whether there had been three shots fired or four. The defense position was that there were only three, with the third shot wounding Carlos in the back bench seat, then exiting through the window. The prosecution maintained that there had been four, with Carlos exiting the car, shooting the third shot through the window, then carefully shooting himself with the fourth—the bullet that was lost, along with one shell casing.

As for a fourth shot, Harper stated that there should have been one more shell casing found and also an impact mark in the asphalt where the blood and the shell casing had been found.

In his cross-examination of Dr. Harper, ADA Perrone got the defense witness to admit that it was not uncommon for forensic experts to fail to find bullets and shell casings at crime scenes.

The prosecution had requested and received Harper's notes and observations. The notes were on his laptop. The district attorney's IT expert lifted the notes off the hard drive and provided a hard copy for the prosecution. Perrone kept the defense witness on the stand for two hours going over all his observations.

There was one glaring omission in the notes that Harper had not addressed in open court: the fact that he had not found any blood on the rear bench seat where the defense claimed Carlos had been shot. Portale immediately objected to the prosecution's entry of the notes to the court record, arguing that they were inadmissible evidence. Judge

Zambelli sustained his objection and had them struck from the record, advising the jury to ignore the exchange regarding the notes. But the observation had become a hanging question that would not be answered, and something that could only hurt the defense.

CHAPTER THIRTY:

"ENFLAME PREJUDICE"

AFTER THE OBLIGATORY attempt by defense to have Judge Zambelli declare a mistrial failed, the jury was called in. McClure took his place behind the podium that faced the jury. He characterized the prosecution's case not as "Murder 101," as ADA Christine O'Connor did in the People's opening remarks, but as "Creative Writing 101." McClure told the jury that Carlos Perez-Olivo had been the "second gunshot victim" out on Route 100 the night of November 18, 2006. The People's circumstantial case against him was nothing more than "innuendo and speculation."

For the next two hours, McClure rebutted all the major witnesses for the prosecution. As for the theory that Carlos was broke and needed the money from his wife's life insurance policies, McClure said that Carlos wasn't even aware of the existence of some of them, since his wife had paid the premiums, and he had no idea of the payoff amounts involved.

McClure told the jury that they had to look at the credits and the debits of his banking accounts, and not the ending balances of every month. The high-profile criminal cases were usually paid in cash, and there was his Venezuelan oil venture and the mysterious trips to Canada. McClure again was suggesting that some of Carlos' income was undeclared. His ability to pay the astronomical rents in affluent Chappaqua, the tuition for his three kids' college educations, and maintaining the family's five cars was proof that the defendant was not destitute.

The disgraceful tactic of "dragging into court" his former mistress was another attempt to "inflame prejudice" against the man on trial. The extramarital affair, McClure reminded the jury, had been over for a year and a half.

Zoning in on the testimonies of the star witness for the prosecution, Mark Gazzola and his father Giancarlo, Mc-Clure said they were "incredible and inconsistent." Mark Gazzola was not a gun expert, and the Walther PPK semi-automatic he'd supposedly seen was not a rare firearm, as he'd claimed. The defense's gun expert, Louis Romero, who inspected the murder weapon while on the stand, said the Walther was not a collectible because of the mismatched serial numbers on the frame and slide, and would be of no value to him.

McClure claimed that the November trip into the city was not some kind of nefarious plan, but as Carlos and Peggy's kids had testified, simply a common routine of their parents.

The defense counsel insisted that their experts had proven that there were just three shots, not four as the People were insisting. The medical examiner who'd testified in court had not even been at the autopsy, but had somehow come to his conclusion by viewing photographs! He was wrong about the stippling, argued McClure, mistaking hair follicles as gunshot residue. Peggy's wound proved that she had not been executed, but tragically shot in the struggle for the gun.

As for the recovered gun, McClure said Barney Fife—the inept deputy on the 1960s sitcom *The Andy Griffith Show*—could have found it in Echo Lake after being directed to the spot by his client. The defense attorney concluded by reminding the jury that their expert witness, Dr. Harper, had determined that the fatal wound had not been an execution shot, but a stray bullet that had gone tragically awry.

The prosecution's closing remarks began the next morning, Friday, October 3, the twelfth day of the trial.

ADA Perry Perrone said the people had proven their case by showing that Perez-Olivo had been on a "downward spiral," and that Carlos' solution had been to kill his wife. That, Perrone said, would have to be the "inescapable conclusion" of the jury.

Perrone lost little time in reviving star witness Mark Gazzola's testimony. Gazzola, a volunteer witness, "saw what he saw," and that was the murder weapon, the .32-caliber Walther PPK, in the possession of the defendant just four months prior to the murder. Gazzola's father, Giancarlo, was there too, and confirmed his son's account of the exchange he'd had with the accused.

Just three months before the murder of his wife, Carlos had been stripped of his license to practice law. He had lost his livelihood, a livelihood that his lawyer son Carlitos, Perrone said, wanted nothing to do with. His children, by their own admission in testimony, didn't find out about the disbarment until after the murder of their mother. The only one who did know was Ileana Poole, Carlos' mistress for most of the past ten years. Ileana's birthday fell on November 18. Carlos hadn't forgotten; he had sent flowers.

Why did Carlos ditch the gun in such an obvious place? Because after shooting his wife, he couldn't chance holding on to it and disposing of the weapon later for fear of being caught with it. He had to get rid of the gun at the murder scene, and that was one reason why he picked the remote spot on Route 100 next to the lake to pull over and execute his sleeping wife.

Was it really a long throw of the pistol into the lake for the 58-year-old man? Perrone expressed his doubt by reminding the jury that the accused was a regular at Club Fit, where he worked out and played rigorous games of pick-up basketball.

As for the mysterious Colombian hit man, Carlos had told three variations of the attack. None of them, said the ADA, made any sense.

Why, after running the Montero off the road, didn't the "hit man" just shoot him through the window? The two other guys? Why didn't they get out of their vehicle? Why didn't the attacker say something: some demands if it was a carjacking or a stick-up? Why didn't he punch Carlos when Carlos had his two hands on his wrist in the struggle for the gun? And Peggy slept through all this? What about the fact that there was no blood found on the back seat—neither his nor the intruder's?

Then there was the undisturbed water bottle in the center console, and the lack of scuff marks on the dashboard from the struggle. How do you explain the plastic bag in his overcoat with gunpowder residue? The bullet in the roof liner with the trajectory indicating it had been shot from the driver's seat and not from the back, where the struggle allegedly took place? Ballistics also showed that the bullet hole in the car window was a result of firing the handgun at it in a 90-degree angle while outside the vehicle. That would explain why the lead projectile and shell casing were not found. Carlos' wound? It was a superficial one that was carefully placed so no major organs would be hit. His wound was part of the plan to eliminate himself as a suspect.

Finally Perrone addressed the dramatic 911 call. Perrone pointed out that Carlos had told the dispatcher that he'd been shot right up front, and it wasn't until fifty seconds into the call that his mortally wounded wife was mentioned. Ninety seconds into the tape, he said his wife had been "murdered." How did he know she was dead? Why didn't he pull over, like the 911 operator had told him to, and wait for medical attention that could have reached him in just minutes?

Perrone sat down after almost three hours of summarizing the People's case against Carlos Perez-Olivo. Although their case against him was purely circumstantial, it was a strong one.

CHAPTER THIRTY-ONE:

DAY OF RECKONING

AFTER BEING BRIEFED by Judge Zambelli on the finer points of law as it pertained to them, the jurors, who had been sequestered the night before, were tasked to reach a verdict on whether Carlos Perez-Olivo was guilty of murdering his wife.

Huddled in their jury room, they made a few requests: they wanted to hear the 911 tape again, and they wanted to see the murder weapon and the photograph of the defendant's left hand with the abrasion on his thumb-forefinger webbing. It appeared that viewing the murder weapon and the photo of the hand might help them determine if Carlos had fired the gun, and whether the design of the pistol could easily cause "slide bite"—when the slide blows back to eject a shell casing, it can tear into an improperly placed hand, causing an abrasion or "bite."

The jury was still deliberating when Judge Zambelli called it a day at 6 PM. Assembled back in the courtroom, she told them that they would be asked to pick up where they'd left off the next morning, a Saturday, at 9 AM.

The morning deliberations created a deadening lull for those waiting for a verdict. By 1 PM most had drifted off to get a bite to eat, leaving only a few in the lobby reading a book or newspaper, or pecking away on their laptops and BlackBerrys. It was looking like a long day ahead when suddenly court officers spread the news that a note from the jury had been delivered to Judge Zambelli. After eight and a half hours of deliberations, the jury had reached a unanimous decision.

When Perez-Olivo was returned to the courtroom from his holding cell, he made a quick scan of the gallery for family and friends. Finding none, his usually expressionless face morphed into a look of resigned disappointment.

Word of the verdict had yet to spread beyond the walls of the courthouse. Judge Zambelli, nevertheless, ordered the jurors to return to the courtroom without delay and announce their decision. McClure and Portale hadn't had time to call any of the Perez-Olivo family to tell them a verdict was in, since they themselves had had to rush back to court in time to hear the verdict. Zambelli warned that she would not tolerate any outbursts in court once the verdict was announced.

After standing for the arrival of the jury, the collection of reporters and other onlookers stared hard at the faces of the seventeen jurors for some expression or show of body language that indicated relief, anger, sympathy or guilt, telegraphing their decision. None could be discerned. The jurors sat and looked to Judge Zambelli. She asked the foreman, Juror Number One, if they had reached a decision on the two charges the defendant faced. The middle-aged Caucasian woman stood and said they had.

Zambelli asked as to the first charge of second-degree murder, what was their verdict?

"Guilty," the foreman said.

Judge Zambelli got the same response to the charge of illegal possession of a dangerous weapon. Perez-Olivo simply nodded his head as if it was the decision he'd expected.

At the request of the defense, the jury was polled individually for their decision. Once the verdict was confirmed, Judge Zambelli thanked them, then formally excused the seventeen men and women. The court, Zambelli announced, would reconvene on December 3, 2008, for sentencing.

Perez-Olivo, without being told, extended his hands behind his back and was quickly handcuffed by a court officer. Not a sound could be heard from the gallery as they watched the convicted man being led away. Perez-Olivo gave one more glance over his left shoulder at the spectators, his age-lined, swarthy face devoid of emotion. He was looking for a friendly sympathetic face. He found none.

When the surprise announcement came down that the jury had reached a decision, Merced was up in Chappaqua at a buddy's house and reached by Portale on his cell phone. No one was expecting a quick decision from the sequestered jury.

Racing back to White Plains, Merced leapt out of the car and, in his business suit, sprinted for the courthouse.

"I was running for the steps," Merced recalled, "and I see all our lawyers and experts stop in their tracks and just look at me. Rich Portale said, 'I'm sorry, but they found him guilty.' I couldn't believe it. It was like someone pulled a joke on me. Just a huge sick joke. It took about twenty seconds to sink in. There was no emotion, just shock. I started walking to the stairs when I caught a look of myself in those long mirrors, and I looked nice, dressed in a suit and tie. I dressed nice every day, just so the jury could see me respectful and all. But I didn't need the suit anymore, so I ripped off the jacket and threw it downstairs. As soon as I did that, I just blew up. I started punching the wall. I was so enraged, I remember losing my vision. I remember I started hitting the wall until it just caved in."

Portale and McClure tried to calm him down. They didn't want to see him on the evening news. They told him they had to be careful with an appeal in the works, saying his outburst could hurt his father. Merced certainly didn't want to do that. But the rage was slow in ebbing. A wastebasket was sent flying with a swift kick from Merced. He felt a need to destroy, as he was destroyed.

Merced was hustled out through a back door of the courthouse by Portale and McClure, away from the court cops and the media.

On the eighth floor of the courthouse, Westchester County District Attorney Janet DiFiore addressed the assembled press. She talked glowingly about how the investigators had "unraveled Perez-Olivo's bold, bold plan." It was, she said, "an incredible account of what took place that night on the side of the road in Chappaqua."

Several times she made mention of the "outstanding job" the New Castle police had done in the course of the investigation. She had more praise for the rookie homicide detectives: "They uncovered, after a very deliberate, careful, painstaking investigation, a calculat[ed] plan, motivated largely by [Carlos'] greed to kill his wife."

The DA had only superlatives when she thanked ADAs Perry Perrone and Christine O'Connor, the crime lab personnel, the "good citizens that came forward" and the jury.

DiFiore ended her remarks by saying that her office was prepared to ask the court to sentence Perez-Olivo to the full 25-years-to-life sentence for killing his wife.

Lieutenant Detective Marc Simmons stepped forward and added that he wanted to thank the New York State Department of Correctional Services Inspector General's Office, who provided "a tremendous amount of service and assistance" to investigators. When pressed for details, Simmons declined to elaborate, other than to say it was "background information relevant to the case." Simmons then melted back into the crowd on the dais.

Simmons would later explain that the Inspector General's Office had helped "facilitate interviews between us [NCPD] and some inmates in prison, including Tony Stevens. In addition, they provided some background info on these inmates."

TV reporters peppered the detective with more questions. Simmons, in response to one question about their initial suspicions, said the attack on that road had gotten their attention because it was in itself unusual; nothing like that had ever happened in the area before. There were also a number of smaller issues, he said, that were raised "that didn't check out."

"When you put it in the totality of circumstances, that's

why it began not to smell right," Simmons related. "It wasn't one individual thing, but small things put together."

A reporter asked if he was referring to the insurance policies. He replied no, it was something about the date of the murder. "It was a date that was significant to Mr. Perez-Olivo," he said.

Prodded for more details, Simmons reluctantly said that the murder had taken place on the birthday of Mr. Perez-Olivo's former mistress, Ileana Poole. It was a coincidence that couldn't be ignored. It had detectives taking a harder look at Mr. Perez-Olivo.

CHAPTER THIRTY-TWO:

MAN FRIDAY

IF THERE WAS one person who knew Carlos better than anyone—even better than Peggy—it was Rolando (name changed here at his request). Carlos calls Rolando his "right-hand man, his man Friday, his son." Both men claimed to have no secrets between them. Rolando says he loves Carlos like a father and would do anything for him. What has happened to his mentor has made Rolando an angry man. Rolando says Carlos is not a murderer, but a gentleman who could never hurt anyone. That he could kill Peggy was beyond ridiculous.

The native New Yorker admits to having been on both sides of the law. As a kid he had gotten involved with some Italian mobsters in his neighborhood, got arrested, was convicted and served some time in a federal penitentiary. After getting out of prison, Rolando enrolled at John Jay College in Manhattan and attended for two years, but had to drop out and go to work before he earned a degree in criminal justice.

He met Carlos in 1999. Rolando had a paralegal friend at a law office in Queens that Carlos had a space in. The friend started up an immigration practice with Carlos, and Rolando was brought in to do some computer work.

Carlos knew Rolando wasn't making much money servicing office computers, so he asked the hard-working Hispanic if he'd like to do some "footwork" for him. Since Rolando had aspirations of becoming an attorney, he jumped at the chance of working for a practicing lawyer. It was the kind of practical experience he was looking for. The two of them, according to Rolando, "hit it off," and after a few months, did well enough to move to a bigger office in Sunnyside, Queens. After a falling-out with his partner over some business transactions, Carlos left to open his own office in nearby Kew Gardens. He took Rolando with him. Business was good.

Carlos taught him how to prepare motions and other legal procedures, the kind of work that paralegals perform, the 30-year-old explained. Rolando also rounded up clients for his boss.

When things were slow, Rolando would put on his suit and go down to night court and "scare up some business."

"Because I looked the part, people would come up to me and ask in Spanish if I was a lawyer. I'd hit it off with them and tell them no, I wasn't a lawyer, but I worked with an attorney and here is his card. Ninety percent of our clients were Spanish," Rolando related.

Most of the work they got was by referral. Rolando says Carlos had a lot of empathy with the Spanish community, and did a lot of *pro bono* and reduced rate work for them. "Carlos," Rolando said, "had a lot of heart."

Rolando did not know Peggy well, although he did do a lot of work for her, mostly when her computer was acting up and with things that needed to be done around the house that Carlos didn't have time for.

Rolando said that Carlos and Peggy had a great relationship. He never saw them fight or raise their voices at each other, nor did he hear Carlos ever complain about her. According to Rolando, they had a "storybook marriage."

"They were very happy people and had a great lifestyle together. They blew money though, always on vacation together, three or four times a year. Whatever she wanted, Carlos would get her."

The NCPD investigators considered Rolando, among other things, Carlos' "bagman." It was something Rolando never really disputed. Rolando knew all about his "stashes," saying with a knowing laugh that Carlos always had cash, and plenty of it. It was a fact that PI Danny Marrone found to be true when he went over Carlos' financials in behest of his defense team.

Marrone, for the most part, substantiated what Rolando claimed, that most of the money came from his criminal law clients, who always paid in cash.

According to Rolando, Carlos couldn't understand why he'd been brought up on charges by the Appellate Division's Disciplinary Committee. He had insisted that he had been truthful in his testimony before the committee. Why didn't they believe him instead of the criminal element he had for clients?

Rolando said his boss was noticeably relieved when he was finally disbarred. He was fed up with the work, the tired and inept criminal law system and the ingrates he worked for.

"He was like a new man when it was over," Rolando remembered.

Rolando was convinced that the Westchester District Attorney and the NCPD believed there was no reason to mount an exhaustive investigation, since, from the very start, they were undissuadably sure that Carlos had murdered his wife.

There was one particular felon who was a strong candidate for ordering a hit on Carlos. According to Rolando, a "heavy-duty" Colombian drug lord/hit man, who was up on a federal death penalty charge in Kansas City, was "pissed off" that Carlos had bowed out of his case. As far as Rolando knew, the authorities had never looked into the possibility that the Colombian might have made good on his threats.

Rolando explained that the mentality of many of their clientele was that they paid Carlos to get them off—and in the Third World, where they came from, when you paid a lawyer, you got off. Those who were convicted felt cheated, and that lent itself to the threats made against Carlos' life. "These were guys who could make good on threats too!" Rolando said.

"They didn't talk to me about the threats I got," Rolando bitterly recounted. "They didn't talk to the guy in Westchester

[Bob Wright] who had the same thing happen to him. They had their guy [Carlos], and that was it."

Elio Cruz was a strong suspect as well, said Carlos' associate. In a stunning revelation, Rolando claims Cruz did not shoot his wife's lover, which he was convicted of, but had paid a relative to kill him, a worse crime in the eyes of the law.

In Cruz's uneducated mind—twisted by jealousy and revenge—he was not responsible for the murder, since he did not pull the trigger, even though he was just as guilty for hiring the hit man.

"Then his family starts calling in threats to Carlos. I took a lot of those calls!"

Rolando disputes the claim by the DA that Carlos was broke. When Carlos was arrested, Rolando says, he was holding $75,000 in cash for Carlos. Rolando had asked him if he needed it, and Carlos had told him no, he had more cash at home.

Private Investigator Marrone says Rolando was right about Carlos' financial situation. In his examination of his accounts he found that Carlos regularly made large deposits and withdrawals.

"They were not two- or three-thousand-dollar sums, but forty, fifty thousand. Not exactly chump change," Marrone related.

When he got the call from Carlitos that Carlos and Peggy had been shot, Rolando thought he was joking because of Carlitos' matter-of-fact delivery. Not having a car, Rolando had to wait two hours for a friend to drive him up to the Mount Kisco hospital.

He was with attorney Buckley when he walked into Carlos' room. They found Carlos distraught, crying that he was to blame, that it was his enemies who had done this to him and Peggy, and that he should have protected her.

Rolando, along with Frank Furillo, spent two weeks sleeping at the foot of Carlos' bed with a sword, baseball bat and Merced's pit bull. Carlos, according to his protégé, was "out of it," and stayed in bed much of the time. That Carlos was putting on an act was ludicrous to Rolando.

"If you were there, you would see the man was clearly devastated. And Carlos was a macho guy who didn't like to show his emotions."

As far as the Gazzolas as witnesses were concerned, Rolando believes they'd lied, plain and simple.

"For one thing, they testified that Carlitos was there. He wasn't. I was. Do I look like I'm a six' two" guy? [as Carlitos is—Rolando is 5' 8"]. Also, I personally inspected the whole house before we left. There were no boxes left behind. There was no gun on the floor of that bedroom, or in any closet."

According to Rolando, it was he who drove Carlos to the house on Devoe Road to retrieve the $18,000 he had forgotten. He said Carlos was gone for just two to three minutes. When he came back, he had the money and a pellet gun that used to belong to Rolando until he'd given it to Merced.

"It was not a real gun; it was my old pellet gun," Rolando insisted.

Rolando wanted to testify, but defense attorney McClure did not think his testimony was needed. Also, Rolando had a criminal record. Witness credibility issues would have been detrimental to their case, and the defense team decided it was unwise to have him take the stand.

CHAPTER THIRTY-THREE:

MONDAY MORNING QUARTERBACKS

"FROM THE VERY beginning, the whole case was screwed up," said Danny Marrone, a former NYPD homicide detective and now a private investigator. He had been brought aboard the Perez-Olivo defense team by Robert Buckley, and retained by McClure, the lead attorney. Marrone did most of the legwork for the defense. He says the defense— Chris McClure, Richard Portale, ballistics expert Mike Archer and himself—were working the case an average of twenty hours a day during the last month leading up to the trial. If they were going to clear their client, they had to find evidence in a mountain of paperwork: 2,000 pages of documents, statements and tip sheets turned over to them by the DA's office in accordance with discovery requirements. Marrone says tempers, egos and turf led to some friction between the players. He also commented that it was common to have some flare-ups with men working hard on a case that had so much riding on it.

Marrone was stupefied at how the 911 call was handled—or rather, mishandled. He finds it difficult to understand why the dispatcher was trying to find out whose jurisdiction they were in instead of simply getting a patrol officer to the scene. When it became clear that Carlos was on his way to the hospital, patrol cops should have been at the hospital awaiting them. Carlos and Peggy were already in the ER being treated by the time the first cops arrived at Northern Westchester.

PI Danny Marrone made an interesting discovery when he went to the crime scene to take some photographs just prior to the start of the trial. He noticed vegetation and tree limbs that once obscured the view of the lake had recently been removed or were cut away, giving one a clear, unobstructed view of the scene. It also would make something like disposing of a handgun relatively easy. Had the obstructive vegetation been left alone, it would have made any attempt to throw something into the water extremely difficult, especially on a dark, moonless night.

Along the length of the lake abutting Route 100, there was no other trimming of vegetation visible. It begged the question, Marrone ruminated, why the area next to the crime scene was the only spot along that stretch of road that had been tidied up. Was someone trying to give the impression that the murderer had an easy toss of the handgun to make? Clearly the heavy cover would make it extremely difficult, if not impossible, for a wounded man to perform such a task.

Marrone believed it was just one more reason to believe that Carlos didn't do it.

"Anyway," he added, "Carlos was way too smart to have made a mistake of disposing the murder weapon in the most obvious place. The guy was a criminal defense attorney! He must have learned a few tricks along the way. There were hundreds of spots along the road where he could have tossed the gun without it ever being found."

The experienced homicide investigator also believes a murderer would never take investigators anywhere near where they had committed the crime.

"Their first course of action would be to throw them off the scent and not lead them by the nose to where they had done the deed. It just doesn't make sense," Marrone said.

To Marrone, the pro-prosecution trace evidence work done by the county crime lab was shoddy, and the ADAs' handling of the case and what he viewed as the obvious anti-defense bias of Judge Zambelli all added up to a case Carlos never had a chance of winning in court.

* * *

Richard Portale made a promising discovery for the defense leading up to the trial. He had dug up some information on Carlos' living arrangements that could have given the Gazzolas a possible motive to lie about the murder weapon. Mark Gazzola had testified that he had seen the Walther PPK in Carlos' possession five months before Peggy's murder.

Portale had learned that Carlos had a "Lease with an Option to Buy" agreement with the property owner, Mario Gazzola, Mark's uncle. The agreement called for a portion of the rent money to go toward the purchase price of the home on Devoe Road. Carlos recollects that when the Option to Buy agreement was negotiated, the rent payable increased from $3,500 to $5,500 per month. But nineteen months into the arrangement, Carlos wanted out, because he was starting to have legal problems that he guessed could eventually lead to his disbarment. Carlos was concerned about moving ahead with the property purchase and not being able to show sources of income if he was suspended or disbarred from practicing law. Any scrutiny by the Internal Revenue Service might raise questions that could be costly.

Although they were pursuing it as a possible motive for the Gazzolas to see to it that Carlos stayed in jail, that theory turned out to be a dead end for the defense. There was indeed an Option to Buy agreement between Carlos and Mario Gazzola. However, according to Mario Gazzola, while the agreement stipulated that a portion of the rent would be credited to the purchase price, it also stated that if Carlos opted out, as he eventually did, no money would be refunded to him. Carlos disputes this point. As far as he was concerned, the agreement was to refund the extra rent money if a sale did not go ahead.

Mario Gazzola now had $38,000 of Carlos' money that Carlos believed he should be obligated to pay back. The problem for the defense was that this information had come from Carlos with no accessible proof of it in writing. That meant if the defense were to enter the Lease with an Option to Buy agreement into the court record, they would have to put Carlos on the stand to testify to its existence. That would then expose Carlos to cross-examination by the prosecution. Mario Gazzola was never called to testify, so the question of the lease remains unanswered. For himself, Carlos does not remember having a signed deal—only a verbal agreement; nor does he recall how much he was due back once he'd opted out of the deal. He is sure in his claim that he never received any money back—but he never tried to get a refund, because he said he felt bad reneging on a handshake deal.

There was, however, supporting evidence discovered by PI Marrone that would back the assertion of the defense that the agreement with Gazzola existed. In the rental prior to Devoe Road, Carlos had a similar arrangement with the landlord of that house. Three years into the deal, the property values skyrocketed in Chappaqua and the landlord decided not to sell, since the agreed-upon purchase price was paltry compared to the readjusted value of the house.

Carlos sued the landlord, but settled out of court for $50,000 in damages, plus the $36,000 he had paid toward the purchase of the house. The Perez-Olivo family then moved into the Gazzola house on Devoe Road. If the defense had been able to enter the information on the prior rental into evidence, it would not be too much of a reach to have the jury accept the possibility that Carlos had entered into a similar agreement with Mario Gazzola. It certainly wouldn't prove that the Gazzolas had a motive to lie—which was the defense's theory but had never been proven—or that they had a motive to see Carlos incarcerated for life. But it could have provided some doubt to jurors. It would take only one juror exercising the reasonable doubt factor to get an acquittal.

Portale had wanted the jury to hear the defense's argument that Mario Gazzola may have owed $38,000 to Carlos. He said that it gave a possible motive to Mark Gazzola to have said what he did. Putting Carlos behind bars would make it difficult to collect any money owed to him.

The defense could not get that information in front of

the jury without Carlos testifying and opening him to cross-examination on, among other things, his disbarment.

McClure believed that the prosecution wanted Carlos' disbarment particulars aired in court because the prosecution could then insist that his disbarment would go to motive: no job, no income. They could then claim that the many insurance policies on Peggy's life would solve that problem.

Carlos' personal knowledge of the law and how it worked meant that from the start he had told his family and friends the authorities would be going after him. He had seen it all the time in his law practice. It was inevitable. And Carlos' reasoning was sound. As a defense lawyer he knew only too well that, statistically, spouses are overwhelmingly responsible for their mates' deaths.

Carlos had always believed that he would be found innocent. "One of the things," he related, "that kept me going was that once we went to trial, this thing would be resolved. I was there, I know what happened, and our forensics proved it. The people who knew us would testify that there was no way in hell I could do this."

Carlos describes himself as a "dinosaur," and not just because he was a solo practitioner of law, but because he felt that if he was in the right, then all would be well. He was wrong, he says.

Carlos believes that because he didn't react properly, because he shouldn't have been where they were the night of November 18, 2006, he is responsible for the tragedy. Philosophically, Carlos thinks this belief has helped him to handle prison better than most. "Intellectually it is stupid, I know," Carlos said, "but emotionally it's hard."

The day before sentencing, December 1, 2008, Carlos related that he had had a difficult week. His daughter Alysia had come down from Canada to visit him in jail. She was upset and crying, saying she needed her dad and wanted him to be around to watch her grow up. He tried to comfort her, telling her that at 19 years of age, she had already grown. All the more so, given the experiences she had gone through over the last two years. Trying to cheer her up just made it all the more difficult for him. He realized, once he saw his daughter and the state of mind she was in, that his own reasons for wanting to be acquitted were very much secondary to the needs of his kids, and it was his parental responsibility to try harder and prove himself innocent.

It was because his children, more than anyone else, knew what kind of a life Peggy and he had had together. They knew he could never hurt her, and it was this fact that made it so difficult for them to deal with the situation. They had placed so much faith in the justice system, and it had failed them, Carlos said. Carlos had to keep the faith to set an example for his kids. Otherwise, he would be sending the message that when things get tough, you quit. He says he couldn't do that to them.

Carlos was torn about addressing the court at sentencing. He wanted to attack the prosecution. But he had second thoughts, wondering, "What would be the point?"

The sentence that Carlos felt sure he would get was 25 years to life. He knew it was going to be hard listening to the prosecution and Judge Zambelli tear him apart in front of his family and friends, and Carlos desperately wanted to be able to defend himself against the terrible charges. But he knew this was not the time, and he could only hope that at some unknown date in the future, he would be given the opportunity.

Carlos believed the Westchester district attorney was a very strong force in the county and some judges were loath to cross. Zambelli's seat was an elective position. Being a maverick would cost her votes—and the DA's support. As a trial attorney, Carlos recognized that the Westchester DA had more influence on how justice was dispensed than most state district attorneys. If he attacked the ADAs for their high-handed ways, it would just give Judge Zambelli more justification for giving him the maximum sentencing— "not that she needed it," he added.

* * *

Chris McClure was bitter about how the trial was handled by the DA's office: "The job of the district attorney's office is to see that justice is done and that they get a fair and just conviction. But for this DA, it is win at any cost. The state has to be held to a higher standard. It's their burden to convict you."

It had been the second or third week after the funeral, in December 2006, when Carlos got his first "big hurt."

He had called his sister-in-law, Joanne. Joanne was Peggy's closest sister. Talking to her was the next best thing to talking to Peggy, because they were so similar. Carlos was understandably shocked and hurt when she told him that she did not want to talk to him, and he was not to call her back. She told her dead sister's husband that she was sad and that she didn't know what to think anymore. Carlos confided the situation initially to his psychiatrist friend, Ira Korner, who advised him that she was probably still in shock and wouldn't know what to think. He advised Carlos to give his sister-in-law more time to heal.

Carlos said that Joanne knew he would never hurt her sister. Innocently, Carlos then made the mistake of telling Detectives Simmons and Vargas of Joanne's refusal to talk to him. He remembers they quizzed him on the subject. He was honest with them and told them that she was blaming him for Peggy's death. He later found out that they had begun calling her. When the grand jury was eventually convened, Joanne was the only sibling of Peggy who was questioned.

After the verdict was in, Peggy's other sister Sissy, who had testified on Carlos' behalf, began to have second thoughts as to her brother-in-law's innocence. Since the jury, who had heard all of the evidence, had come back with the conviction, there must be something to it, she thought.

"It broke my heart," Carlos said when he found out

about her change of mind. "It bothers me when the DA says stupid things, and it bothers me when the press says stupid things, but to have somebody who you care about, that you feel should know better, it really hurts."

Carlos had always been willing to talk to the district attorney, as were his kids. He could have asked them anything he wanted. And Carlos was willing to take a lie detector test. Nobody took him up on his offer.

He denies that he was laundering any money he got in South America. Carlos said that the people he was dealing with "had had problems" with the United States authorities and would not enter the country. That's why Carlos was so valuable. As to his own status with the Internal Revenue Service, he might have had problems, but at the time, he didn't know. He insisted he had nothing to hide and that the money he was paid was earned.

The gun in the lake didn't make much sense. If Carlos was the shooter, why would he direct cops to the crime scene after disposing of the weapon in the most logical place for the authorities to search? If he masterminded this murder, Carlos, says his attorney, certainly would have shown a lot more caution, perhaps disposing of the gun in a place where it would never have been found.

Lieutenant Simmons was not a factor, says McClure, since the prosecution's case hinged on forensics and the Gazzola testimony, both of which Simmons had nothing to do with. That, explains McClure, is why the defense did not challenge Lieutenant Simmons' expertise with respect to his experience in homicide. Many court watchers thought the defense should have raised the issue, especially as they knew that the New Castle detective had never previously led a homicide investigation.

McClure did not believe entering the 911 tape into evidence was a mistake. "The jury would have to have believed that my client faked it, and I honestly still don't think you can believe that after listening to it."

* * *

Forensics expert Mike Archer believed that Chris McClure
had misrepresented himself to Carlos as an experienced
criminal defense lawyer. Yes, McClure had lots of experience as an ADA in the Bronx, but the defense side of a case
was, according to Archer, a "whole different ball game." It
was a cause of contention between the two men. And with
the long hours spent together as they culled through the
mountains of paperwork that made up the discovery, the
situation was only exacerbated, leading to heated arguments
between them.

Archer believed Carlos to be a "smart man" who would
never have killed his wife using a gun that he'd been con-
nected to by a witness just a few months before.

"He was a criminal defense attorney," said Archer, "and
he knew a lot of bad people, and with one phone call could
have had a trunkful of guns he would never have been con-
nected to. The Gazzolas may have seen a gun, but it was not
the gun."

Archer said that Carlos' purported dire financial status
as a result of being disbarred was the element of the case that
must have figured most prominently in his conviction: "Did
the life insurance fund the defense?" Archer rhetorically
asked. "Remember that Carlos was able to support his lifestyle, the $5,500-a-month rent, the five cars, etc., for thirteen
months following Peggy's death. He was not a pauper—
despite what the People [prosecution] want you to believe.
Everybody knows he has money outside the country. There is
nothing sinister about this—he was outside of the country a
lot of the time. Another point to consider: Carlos was out of
the country after the shooting. If he was guilty—why didn't
he flee then?"

Carlos believes that it was "abundantly clear" that money
wasn't an issue. He says that the deposits that were made to
the accounts show that he wasn't broke.

The defense team's decision that he not testify on his
own behalf was a difficult one to make. If he took the stand,
Zambelli's decision would allow the prosecution to question
him about his disbarment and his affair with Ileana Poole in

their cross-examination, so he opted not to. Although the defense team believed the issues were arguable and had no bearing on the murder charges, they knew they would have been prejudicial to their client. Carlos had wanted to testify, since he knew that juries always want to hear from the accused. Keeping silent suggests guilt.

Archer questioned the People's contention that there were no scuff marks on the Montero's dashboard. Archer said that there *were* scuff marks, and they took photos of them and presented them to the defense's forensics witness, Dr. Harper. The prosecution claimed they'd been made when the car was disassembled by the crime lab after the shootings. But, said Archer, there was no notation by the lab indicating who, where and how the marks were made. Archer claims the lab had altered the evidence by their clumsy work. They also had no photographs of their own of the scuff marks. "It makes you wonder why," he said.

Why the defense didn't press the issue was a question only Chris McClure could answer, said Archer.

Brandi Benjamin, the crime lab's forensic scientist, testified before the grand jury that the water bottle in the center console was "pristine, as if it came from the manufacturer." Not true, says Archer. "The water bottle was dented and bent forward. Every indication of some sort of struggle."

Archer said that Lieutenant Detective Simmons never investigated credible sources who'd sworn that Carlos had been threatened by Latin Kings gang members. In one instance, claims Archer, an FBI confidential informant overheard some Latin Kings members talk about getting some lawyer and his wife.

Archer also said there was a second report from a credible source that said there was still another former client of Carlos with links to the Latin Kings who had a past history of shootings. "At best," said Archer, "Detective Simmons did a cursory review of that evidence."

The defense claims the "slide bite" on Carlos' left hand

was a defensive wound gotten during the struggle for the gun in the SUV. Why, Mike Archer asks, would Carlos fire just once with his left hand? "The slide bite is as equally consistent with Carlos grabbing the gun and being cut by it."

Archer was also critical of Portale and McClure for their failure to bring to the jury's attention that Peggy was not sleeping, but possibly passed out from the alcoholic drinks she'd imbibed in the city. Archer says she had a blood-alcohol level of .06 when she was brought to the hospital that night. A .08 is legal intoxication when operating a motor vehicle and a .04 is "impaired." To Archer, that would explain why Peggy was "asleep" through the whole altercation.

The blood droplets found outside the car are consistent with Carlos' claims that he walked around the car at the crime scene. They do not, says Archer, prove he shot himself there.

Archer claims there was blood found on the rear bench seat. It just was not enough to extract any DNA from and to pinpoint who it came from.

Archer says he was not impressed by the lack of "pooling of blood" on the back seat, due in part to the position Carlos was in, and to the two shirts he was wearing. When he got out of the vehicle, the collecting blood would have been able to spill out.

There was also a big question mark over Peggy's wound. "There was no stippling," Archer adamantly insisted. It was also "telling" to Archer that the ADAs did not rebut the defense's Dr. Andrew, who had challenged the stippling contention by the People through the chief medical examiner for Westchester County, Dr. Hyland.

Independent solicited expertise also cast a shadow of a doubt over the stippling opinion. Vernon J. Geberth, a well-known homicide expert, was later asked to study the photographs of Peggy's wound. He agreed with the defense's assertion that there was no stippling present.

* * *

In regard to the testimony of Ileana Poole, the fact that the affair had ended eighteen months before Peggy's murder should have negated her testimony. Just because Carlos had been involved in an extramarital fling didn't mean he'd committed more serious crimes.

"Carlos should have testified," Archer said. "Carlos is likeable and his story is believable. I think the jury would have thought differently of him and his version of the events. Being a disbarred attorney, a tax cheat, having a girlfriend, etc., does not make one a murderer. Carlos' famous neighbor shares some of these titles and his wife is still alive. It takes a desperate man to shoot his wife in the head and himself in the abdomen. Despite his station in life, I am not sure Carlos is that man."

CHAPTER THIRTY-FOUR:

NUMBER ONE SUSPECT

CHIEF ROBERT BREEN says Carlos Perez-Olivo wasn't their primary suspect until Mark Gazzola came forward with the story of the Walther PPK handgun. Breen says his department didn't make assumptions based on statistical evidence that a spouse is usually the perpetrator when their husband or wife is the victim of violence.

"When you have a case like this, you have to be very open-minded," He explained. "God forbid you start jumping to conclusions and say, 'It's always the husband.' Within days of the murder, I had people coming up to me in the street telling me, 'You know he did it, right?' Well, I would tell them, 'No, I don't know.'"

Detective Simmons reported directly to Chief Breen, and the two men worked closely together on a daily basis. Breen, who always loved detective work, had a lot of input, but Simmons was the guy in the field. He directed the case and had carte blanche to do whatever he needed to do and go wherever he needed to go, Breen said.

"Marc Simmons had a list of suspects like the Westchester phone book. There were a lot of people we had to eliminate as suspects. He [Carlos] was on our list, but he wasn't our key man up and until we arrested him after Gazzola stepped forward."

According to the defense's forensics guy, Mike Archer, that is "bullshit." Archer had a client who was a cop in another police department who, Archer claims, saw Simmons later the night of the shooting. Said Archer: "Simmons right from the get-go saw Carlos as the leading suspect, and told my source so by saying, 'He's our guy.' "

Breen told his detectives that if they needed help, all they had to do was ask. "This case," said the chief, "was that important." Since the town is the residence of a former President of the United States and a sitting United States Senator, the department was under the media's microscope.

The detectives did utilize a lot of the resources that were available. The county crime lab, the New York State Police, the FBI and the Bureau of Alcohol, Tobacco and Firearms were all tapped for assistance.

Once the gun was found by the state police divers, the NCPD detectives made an exhaustive search of the gun's history.

"It took a lot of time," Breen said of the search.

The serial numbers turned up nothing after a long protracted search.

"The gun was a key piece of evidence," Breen related. "Finding out who owned that gun was critical. When Mark Gazzola came forward and linked Mr. Perez-Olivo to it, [that] was the clincher."

Evidently, although the defense had hoped to undermine the Gazzolas' credibility on the gun issue, they never succeeded before the jury.

The NCPD had some problems of their own that threatened, if not their effectiveness, then certainly the public's confidence in their department. The scandal-loving tabloid, the *New York Post*, opined that "a major obstacle in their quest to bring a killer to justice is their own police department."

Then New York State Attorney General Eliot Spitzer initiated an investigation into the NCPD for an alleged pension scam masterminded by one of the senior officers in the department, Lieutenant John Vize. The attorney general's office claimed that Vize and Officer Dennis Mahoney ran the scam that may have involved up to 25 percent of the town's forty-two-member force.

The alleged plot allowed Mahoney to retire with a pension in 2000 after nineteen years of service instead of twenty. *The Westchester Guardian* reported that twenty years' worth of documents were seized from the New Castle Police Department in 2003 by the Public Integrity Bureau of the office of Westchester District Attorney Jeanine Pirro. The paper claimed that Lieutenant Vize was also involved with arranging shifts under Mahoney's name, referred to by some of the department's members as "Mahoney days."

Attorney General Spitzer filed a civil lawsuit on July 27, 2006, against the two officers, seeking to recover damages of $100,000 and more than $180,000 in pension funds paid out by the State of New York since 2000, as well as salary and benefits paid to Vize by the town during the period of the alleged breach of fiduciary duty from on or about August 1999 to on or about July 2000, as a result of a "paper trail more than a mile wide," according to the *Guardian*. "Tension permeates the New Castle Town Hall as a result of this lawsuit and others that have been brought against the town," the newspaper reported.

Adding to that tension was the issue that town police officers had been working without contracts. Some of the New Castle policemen were even picketing in Chappaqua's downtown business district in order to draw attention to what they say was the town's refusal to negotiate in good faith. Lieutenant Vize, a union trustee, said the town had plenty of money in their budget to give to their policemen, adding, "This town is loaded. They know it, we know it."

Regarding the pension scam, the New Castle Town Board, following their own evaluation of the allegations, concluded that the charges were baseless, and retirement health benefits continued to be paid to Mahoney.

There was more controversy surrounding the department. A Jewish police officer was suing the town and the department for anti-Semitism. Steven Kaufman, who had been employed by the department for twenty-three years, claimed that despite receiving good reviews throughout his career, he could never advance because the top five positions in the NCPD have been held by individuals of Irish heritage, including Chief Breen, Lieutenant James Baynes, Lieutenant John Vize, Lieutenant Charles Ferry, Detective Sergeant James Carroll, and Detective Sergeant Marc Simmons.

Kaufman alleged, in a story that appeared in a local newspaper, that the NCPD "systematically excluded police officers of non-Irish national origin from top positions in the Department which has also created and perpetrated a hostile work environment against Kaufman."

Kaufman also claimed that because of his suit he had been the subject of anti-Semitic insults by other Irish police officers in the presence of commanding officers who did nothing to prevent them, and in fact rewarded those who uttered the remarks.

On June 24, 2005, a petition against the Town of New Castle and the NCPD and named individuals was filed by then Police Officer Steve Kaufman. His lawsuit alleged discrimination in promotions and a hostile work environment, both because of his religion and because he had filed worker compensation claims.

A month later, in July 2005, the Town of New Castle applied a disciplinary charge with 122 specifications against Steve Kaufman. He denied the charges, which alleged among other things that, while on disability leave, he'd participated in activities as a volunteer firefighter, which demonstrated his ability to work a light-duty assignment for the police department.

On June 6, 2007, following a recommendation and report of a hearing, Officer Kaufman was found guilty of forty-two specifications of misconduct, and his position as a police officer with New Castle Police Department was terminated.

On November 18, 2008, the Appellate Division, Second Department upheld the decision, also stating that there was "evidence in the record to support the hearing officer's determination that the disciplinary charges were not preferred against the petitioner as retaliation for his commencement of a civil action against the Town and members of the police department."

The *New York Post* quoted a "high-level prosecutor" who said the suits against the NCPD could be a problem for the department: "There's no question that any defense attorney worth his salt will attack the department. They're definitely going to get wiped all over the place."

Defense Attorney Chris McClure was aware of the suits against the NCPD, but decided they were irrelevant to the Perez-Olivo case. McClure said bringing to the jury's attention the legal problems the department was having might have "backfired in their faces," since the pension scam and the bias case had nothing to do with the department's homicide investigation of his client, Carlos Perez-Olivo.

"We chose not to distract the jury with needless nonsense," McClure said. "The case hinged on forensics and these suits had nothing to do with that. It would have been a distraction that could have hurt us, due to the technical nature of the critical testimony. It was a tactical decision we made."

Chief Breen said the Perez-Olivo case was a very hard investigation and it was a very important case to the NCPD. The retired chief summed it up this way: "He did it. He killed her. That was his gun. He shot himself and threw the gun in the lake. We found the gun, and proved it to be the murder weapon, and [we found] a witness to put it in his hand. Case closed!

"In my opinion, it was a cold-blooded murder. This guy Perez-Olivo took his wife to the city, took her to a movie, took her to dinner, drove thirty miles, pulled over, got in the back seat and shot her in the back of the head while she slept. There's no doubt in my mind that he did it, and it was confirmed by a jury of his peers. I can't give enough credit to Marc and his team. They did a great job with the help of the county, the state police, the FBI and ATF. Perez[-Olivo] thought that he was going to commit the perfect crime, lay it on someone else and walk away with the insurance money. It didn't work. This guy [Perez-Olivo] is a pathological liar, you can't believe anything he says. He had his opportunity to testify in court that he was innocent, and he didn't. That tells you something. If there is a heaven and a hell, he'll burn in hell."

ONE DARK NIGHT

to Mays and his team. They'd a great job with the help of the county; the state police, the FBI and ATF. Fossel Olivo thought that he was going to commit the perfect crime, lay it on someone else and walk away with the insurance money. It didn't work. It never works," he concluded. "Anyone who would commit such a heinous crime as this is probably going to suffer in some way. If he hasn't already, he didn't. That tells you this person is probably going to spend, hell, half a lifetime in hell."

CHAPTER THIRTY-FIVE:

THE WORDS, NOT THE MUSIC

AFTER THIRTY YEARS of marriage, three children, several homes, careers and a life full of shared experiences and memories, you murder your mate? Is it possible—and who could do such a cold, heartless thing?

A sociopath/psychopath for one. Devoid of a conscience, arrogant, a user of people and possessing a sense of entitlement, sociopaths/psychopaths are the scourge of our society. If Carlos were a sociopath, would it explain the murder of Peggy Perez-Olivo in Chappaqua? Probably not, says one expert in the field of criminal psychology.

Shayne Jones, PhD is an associate professor in criminology at the University of South Florida. His specialty is sociology with a focus on criminology. He has studied the subject for twelve years.

Jones explains that the difference between psychopathy and sociopathy, in its simplest form, is that psychopaths are born. That is, there appears to be a biological aspect. One of the more recent theories is dysfunction of a region of the brain called the amygdala. The amygdala is responsible for the processing of emotions and learning, among other things. There is also some speculation that low fear and arousal are its biological underpinnings.

Sociopaths, in contrast to psychopaths, are created by their environment; typically poor parenting (not monitoring/ supervising, and being lax in punishment). The behavior of these two "classes" can be quite similar; the difference lies in the biological (including genetic) predisposition.

The most widely used clinical measure of psychopathy

is the Psychopathy Checklist—Revised (created by Robert Hare). It contains two factors. The first factor has two facets, *interpersonal* and *affective*. Here are the specific items used to score these dimensions:

> ### Interpersonal
> *Glib/superficial*
> *Grandiose sense of self-worth*
> *Manipulative/cunning*
> *Pathological lying*
>
> ### Affective
> *Lacks remorse*
> *Shallow affect*
> *Callous/lacks empathy*
> *Failure to accept responsibility for one's actions*

The second factor (which is more common among criminals) also has two facets, *behavioral* and *antisocial*:

> ### Behavioral
> *Parasitic lifestyle*
> *Lack of realistic long-term goals*
> *Impulsive*
> *Irresponsible*
> *Need for stimulation*
>
> ### Antisocial
> *Poor behavioral control*
> *Early behavioral problems*
> *Juvenile delinquency*
> *Extensive criminal history (as an adult)*
> *Parole violations*

Two additional items, sexual promiscuity and many short-term marital relationships, round out the twenty-item measure (but do not fit in the four aforementioned dimensions).

Each of the twenty items is scored 0 (definitely not

present), 1 (may be present), and 2 (definitely present). The "average" criminal scores a 22. To be clinically diagnosed as a psychopath, a person has to receive a score of 30 or more. Using this measure requires specific clinical training. Jones, however, sees very little evidence of Carlos possessing traits on the second factor. On some of the items on the first factor, Carlos might receive a 1 or a 2—but most people will have a 1 or 2 here and there. Jones doubts Carlos would even get a 20.

There are some, including Jones, who believe there are successful psychopaths.

These are individuals who score high on factor one, but low on factor two. Think of Bernie Madoff, Ken Lay, and other white-collar criminals. From what Jones has learned, Carlos doesn't seem to fit this bill. But Jones can't say for sure without a personal interview.

The core feature of a psychopath is an emotional deficit; he can't experience emotion like a normal person. It's not a matter of choosing not to, but rather being incapable of doing so. For psychopaths, people are objects.

"They know the words, but not the music," Jones explained. "Psychopaths know how to put on a good act. They may seem to be sincere, but that's how they lure people in."

Most victims of psychopaths say there is something about them that is "too good to be true." Psychopaths can be very manipulative. It can be difficult to distinguish between what people see and what the psychopath feels.

As noted, they often have many short-term marriage-like relationships. Jones says that Carlos does not seem to have that in his background. The fact that Carlos was in a thirty-year relationship seems to rule him out as a psychopath. Jones says it doesn't make a lot of sense, because what could a psychopath possibly get out of such a long relationship that he could not get from fifteen two-year relationships? Even with the one extramarital affair, Carlos' behavior does not strike Jones as being consistent with psychopathy.

Psychopaths usually move from one job to another, rarely investing time to forward a career. From their perspective, the rest of us are stupid. Why get up early in the morning and work eight hours to get a paycheck when you can use people and accomplish the same things? Arrogance, entitlement and a parasitic lifestyle are typical of a psychopath.

The fact that Carlos appeared calm and detached to the cops isn't really diagnostic. It may just have been his way of dealing with a traumatic experience.

All the friends and family who had contact with Carlos after the shooting reported that he was in an apparent state of shock and befuddlement for several weeks. Jones says that also is not consistent with psychotic behavior: "Psychopaths can put on an act for a short length of time in an attempt to save themselves, but after a while they would revert to their detached selves. They bore easily."

Typically criminal psychopaths are not terribly ashamed of their actions. "They may lie about what they have done," Jones says, "but if there are no consequences, they may show a very different face to their attorney or in an interview than in a courtroom, where they may appear upset but you don't see any tears. Off the record, when there are no consequences, they are much more likely to open up and show their true colors."

Again, this does not fit Carlos' behavior.

A psychopath also would be more likely to testify on his own behalf. Jones says there are clinical indications that psychopaths enjoy lying for the sake of lying. Serial killer Ted Bundy is a good example of this.

Bundy loved getting up in court and making a case for himself by proving the authorities were not as smart as he was. He believed he could persuade a jury to his side. There was an enjoyment he got out of the manipulation.

Jones thinks that if Carlos were a psychopath, despite the advice of lawyers, he would have testified.

Psychopathic individuals tend to externalize blame, and affront would have been the reaction of a psychopath to a guilty verdict. A "Who are these people to judge me?" attitude would be the typical reaction. They would be angry.

Jones says it is common for someone, perhaps a family member, to come forward and say that the psychopathic individual was guilty. Psychopaths have a pattern of behavior. They don't have the control to keep up the façade for years. Jones explains that the psychopath's true colors would surface and be noticed.

Jones listened to the 911 call Carlos made just after being shot: "There appeared to be a genuine panic. What struck me, if anything, was that Carlos never mentioned his own wounds until asked. Instead, he focused continually on his wife. This is not consistent with psychopathy. I also did not think this sounded like it was staged, if for no other reason than it was too chaotic. I would expect someone who planned this out and was psychopathic to have a story he would begin telling. And he didn't."

Dr. Jones thought Merced Perez-Hall's reaction to the guilty verdict was very telling. A psychopath's parenting would be poor and not very loving. He or she would not endear themselves to children, nor earn their loyalty, since psychopathic individuals don't know how to express love. The Perez-Olivo children's love, loyalty and belief in their father's innocence, visibly expressed in court, contradicts what is known in a family with a psychopathic parent.

That Carlos was treated for depression is another reason to doubt he was psychopathic. Typically psychopaths do not get depressed. Their anxiety levels are very low.

The depression that Carlos suffered, says Jones, is the only thing that stands out as a clinical issue.

A depressed individual might reason that he was sparing a loved one a ruined life, but the depressed individual usually kills himself in these cases as well. Depressed individuals act impulsively.

If Carlos murdered his wife, it was nothing if not carefully planned.

In reviewing the case and psychologically interpreting Carlos' life, Jones says there appears to be no evidence of psychopathology or mental illness.

"There doesn't seem to be any indication that he was psychologically off," Jones said. "From what I learned of him, it seems he was pretty much normal. Nothing stands out about him."

Dr. Jones says most homicides involve two individuals who know one another, and have had some level of conflict in the past. Moreover, most violent offenders can probably be characterized as engaging in *reactive aggression.* Reactive aggression occurs when the perpetrator is responding to some perceived threat or slight. They believe they have been mistreated in some way. This has a technical term—*hostile attribution bias*; this denotes that ambiguous stimuli are perceived in a hostile/threatening way. This type of aggression is different from *instrumental aggression,* whereby the perpetrator uses aggression as a means to an end. Psychopathic individuals engage in both reactive and instrumental aggression, whereas sociopaths may engage in only reactive aggression.

So why would Carlos kill his wife? If he is psychopathic, he may have seen that murder was a necessary "evil" to achieve something else (e.g., money, avoiding a messy divorce). Assuming he killed his wife, he may have been reacting to something: perceived infidelity, insulting/disrespectful behavior or something along those lines. Most of the time, reactively aggressive individuals also demonstrate emotional volatility—they have a temper, become easily angered, can be impulsive and generally disinhibited, and are easily wounded, hurt or frustrated. They are not so much cold and calculating (at least with their aggression), but their emotions get the best of them and they fail to consider the negative consequences. These sorts of things can be gauged by examining the individual's personality, even if informally, by asking people who knew him.

Dr. Jones suspects that if Carlos killed his wife, he would have had to engage in some degree of depersonalization. This refers to experiencing the sensation that one is not in control of his own body, seeing the actions he is perpetrating as being controlled by some unknown force: an out-of-body experience.

"He would have also likely objectified his wife in some manner. In other words, she is not his loving wife of thirty years, the mother of his children, but something that has to be eliminated, like an annoying fly or frightening snake. These psychological actions would almost have had to be in play. Even serial killers report these experiences/perceptions."

CHAPTER THIRTY-SIX:

THE LOVE OF A SON

MERCED PEREZ-HALL IS Peggy and Carlos' middle child, approximately six years younger than Carlitos and six years older than the baby of the family, Alysia. Not as tall or as handsome as his brother, Merced is more of a ruggedly good-looking type. To those who know him, Merced could be said to be defined by his penchant for violent sports, notably ice hockey, wrestling and boxing. His enthusiasm and single-mindedness in his pursuits fairly exudes from his pores.

His father, when he speaks of his middle child, cannot help but exhibit a special pride, if not partiality, to Merced. It's his resolve and passion that impresses his father. Having always wanted to be a soldier, Merced attended West Point.

Despite the love he had for the military, his failure to accept unconditionally the authority of his superior officers had him marching off the demerits he accumulated in the academy's quad on a regular basis. Merced managed to finish that first year unbroken. He wrote about the experience in an essay:

> Just when I thought I'd cleared the hurdle of boot camp, or Beast as they like to call it around West Point; I find that things are getting even more difficult. I have to prove myself all over again to a new group of upperclassmen, and it is going horrible. I am constantly getting hazed, and it seems the more I try to get out of trouble, the more trouble I get in.

*Most of all, when I am not talking to myself, I think
about all the words that are screamed in my face every day. Just quit, you are a failure, you don't belong
here, you're the worst cadet ever, and so on and so
on—these words resonate within my head until it is
all I can hear. Pretty soon, I am not fighting them—
the upper classmen, the officers, and every person
who is trying to make me fail and trying to convince
me to give up—I am fighting myself.*

Finishing that one year at West Point was as good as it was
going to get. It was a small victory, but it was his. He left the
academy on his own terms. The following year, Merced enrolled in the University of Colorado at Boulder, where he
would major in Geography.

Merced was still in the Denver area studying for his
master's degree when he got the call. His brother didn't say
much, only that there had been an accident. Carlitos told
him to get on the next available flight to New York.

Merced loved his mom and dad, and has no memory of either one of them ever raising a hand at him in anger. They
encouraged him in his pursuits and applauded his efforts.
His parents were more best friends than they were authority
figures. His childhood was idyllic.

What he admired most about his parents was their close-
ness and their obvious love for one another. To Merced the
thought that his father could do harm to his mom was just not
in the realm of possibility. He knew his dad would do anything for her, including protecting her at the cost of his own
life. Carlos was an Old World gentleman, where family always comes first.

He found out about his dad's mistress the way the rest of
his family did—in the newspapers. Although disappointed
with his dad's lack of loyalty to his mom, Merced understood
how an unhappy career, family pressure and a midlife crisis
could send a man fleeing into a younger woman's arms. Half

Puerto Rican himself, he acknowledges the age-old wandering eye of the Latin male. His dad was from a world whose culture encouraged men to wink at such dalliances and not condemn them.

In a follow-up call prior to departure for New York, Merced had been told his dad was fine, but his mom was not. Merced still thought they had been involved in an auto accident of some kind—most likely a drunk driver, he told himself. When he saw his brother and a friend gloomily watching his appearance at the arrival gate, he knew immediately that his mother was dead.

Merced has few memories of the week leading up to his mom's funeral in 2006. Like his siblings and his dad, he wandered around in a low level of shock. Merced said the entire family acted like zombies.

The trial proved to be even harder to bear, since they could not attend the legal proceedings on a daily basis: all three children were scheduled to testify for the defense, and witnesses were not permitted to sit and listen to the testimony of others prior to their time in the witness box.

Carlos was adamant about the trial not interfering with their lives, assuring them that he would soon be free, since a verdict of not guilty was, to borrow a gambling term, a "lock."

Their dad's confidence buoyed their spirits and had them convinced that the trial was going their way. Merced echoed this sentiment: "We would all be laughing and eating pizza when this thing was over," he wistfully recalled thinking. "There was just no way they could convict him."

After their testimonies, they were free to attend the rest of the trial. Jurors, other witnesses and the press all agreed that Merced was an effective witness for his dad's defense. The main reason was that the second oldest fervently believed in his father's innocence: "There just is no way in Hell that my dad shot my mom. People that really knew my parents would agree. They were just too much in love, and my dad had too much respect for her. And he never resorted to violence. It just wasn't in his nature."

* * *

Merced says he will never give up on justice for his dad. Giving up hope on his freedom would mean giving up on the man, and he could never do that.

"It's a mutual thing we have, where we are there for each other," Merced said. "My dad has watched his whole life crumble before him. They have taken everything from him, except his fight. And that has given him a reason to carry on."

Merced says that there are a lot of people behind him, and that has given him hope. But, he relates, people who say that at least his dad is still alive just don't understand.

"They don't know any better, since they never had a loved one jailed. Being in prison is no life."

Merced says that people who believe his father killed his mother bother him as much as the fact that his dad sits in jail. "Those people," he says, "don't know my parents, because if they did, they'd know that my dad is incapable of killing my mom, or anybody, for that matter."

According to Merced, there were no facts in his dad's case that prove he did it. It was all circumstantial, with people believing what they wanted to believe.

Despite their far-flung existence from the old Chappaqua days, with Carlitos in Brooklyn, Merced in Colorado and Alysia in Canada, the family stays in touch. They have conference calls every week on Sundays. The siblings all are on the right track—except for him, he says with a bewildered laugh: "I don't know what the hell I'm gonna do. I'm twenty-five years old and I think I'm having a midlife crisis. I want a career, but I don't know what that is. I don't know what I'll be doing, and I don't know where I'll be."

One thing he does know: he'll be living for his father, because that's what his father asked him to do.

CHAPTER THIRTY-SEVEN:

SENTENCING

IN THE TWO months since the start of the trial, the weather had cooled considerably. Gone were the sunny, languid autumn mornings and afternoons. Leaden grey skies and bone-chilling winds now dominated. People no longer lingered outside on the plaza of the courthouse in conversation with friends and colleagues. Pedestrian traffic was swift and direct into the heated corridors where justice waited to be dispensed.

So it was on December 2, 2008.

Carlos Perez-Olivo knew the routine, having had a hand in the machinations of criminal justice for thirty-odd years. Dressed in a dark blue suit, he stood quietly and impassively, his eyes fixed on Judge Zambelli as his moment of judgment had arrived. It had been two years since the crime had occurred that he had been convicted of committing just one month before.

Lawyers waiting to be heard on other cases had filed in and filled the jury box, curious to hear the outcome of the case they had all followed. The jurors were no longer in attendance. They had done their job; the case had been turned over to the presiding judge to put finality to the matter by means of a sentence.

As is his right, Carlos had wanted to address the court before the sentence was passed by Judge Barbara Zambelli, but Chris McClure had talked him out of it. McClure was concerned that his client would be ruled by emotion and perhaps say something that would counter any of their efforts to get an appeal. Also, Carlos, like a lot of attorneys, had a propensity to rattle on long after all cogent points had been made.

ADA Perry Perrone took the floor first. The tall lanky attorney reminded the court that Carlos had been convicted of premeditated murder in the second degree. The murder of Peggy Hall Perez-Olivo had not been committed by an ignorant man, he said. Nor was the crime a product of rage or passion. Carlos was cool and calculating. He was a smart, educated man from a good family. He was not in want of anything growing up. Certainly his background could not be used as an excuse for his actions. Perrone said Carlos was "old," and not some reckless kid. He had known what he was doing.

"If he can commit this crime so late in life, there is no hope for him," Perrone said.

Perrone maintained that Carlos' arrogance was his undoing, since all the evidence pointed to him as the gunman. He thought that he was too clever to be caught. His underestimating of the New Castle police's ability to crack the case was indicative of his huge ego. That, Perrone insisted, was what led to his downfall.

"Perez-Olivo," Perrone added, "manipulated and schemed his children and family. He is the reason why his children have no parents."

This guilty felon pleading for mercy, said the ADA, was a lot like the one who killed his parents and then asked for leniency because he was an orphan. The "insidious nature" of the crime demanded the maximum sentence allowed by law, and the maximum sentence is what the People demanded.

McClure, like Perrone, did not take to the lectern. McClure stood at his seat. The former ADA from the Bronx had a tired, beaten look to him. The long hours in court and the late-night defense sessions spent strategizing had exacted their toll. There were tactical avenues that he and Portale had taken that in retrospect could be second-guessed, but the inescapable fact was, the prosecution had had a strong circumstantial case.

Despite the guilty verdict, Carlos believed McClure and Portale had done a good job. The cards were stacked against him, he believes. Since the day he was arrested, the outcome was never in doubt. He had been tried and found guilty in the media long before a jury was selected. The farcical show of a trial, as orchestrated by the Westchester County District Attorney's office, was just a pro forma exercise, a rubber stamp of what was already decided.

Chris McClure pressed on. He reminded the court that the case against his client was purely circumstantial and "unconvincing." Disagreeing on the verdict, the defense asked the court to at least show some mercy, if not to his client, then to his children, who were now without a parent.

McClure said he'd received countless letters, e-mails and telephone calls from friends and family members of the victim, asking for leniency.

McClure noted that Carlitos was in the courtroom, but that Merced and Alysia were too distraught to attend.

McClure then asked and got permission from Judge Zambelli to read a letter out loud in court that was written by the three children and addressed to the judge:

> *"We are requesting that my father be given the minimum sentence permitted by law for the following reasons:*

> *"My family has been destroyed. We have no mother. Now we have no father. It is impossible to describe the anguish that each of us deals with on a daily basis. We are beside ourselves in grief. We will never be normal again.*

> *"No one has listened to us. We believe our father is innocent. We love him and want him back in our lives. To extend his sentence is to directly extend the pain we experience every day.*

"We trusted the legal system and it has failed us. We are very angry. Our protests have fallen on deaf ears, our misery the subject of the evening news, and our plight pushed aside by politics. We were never given a choice in this matter and we are very angry.

"We want our father to know our grandchildren, walk down the aisle when we marry, and be present in our lives as we achieve further accolades. None of that will happen if you so choose. Please listen to us.

"You have the power to ensure that our father will never be a part of us again. You have the responsibility to choose wisely and prudently. Give us some hope that we may be united with him in the meaningful future. Do not exacerbate this nightmare. Instead, please help my family heal.

"We are victims. We have no power. We are placing our faith in you.

"Please listen to us and give my father the minimum sentence permitted by law.

"The Perez-Olivo family"

Once McClure had finished, Judge Zambelli turned to the convicted murderer. She asked him if he had anything to say. Carlos politely but firmly said no, and that he "was ready for sentencing."

Zambelli lost little time in expressing her beliefs and read from her prepared remarks in an even and emotionless tone:

"The jury verdict in this case leads to one conclusion. The defendant is a master of deceit who contrived a diabolical plan to murder his wife for his own financial gain."

Zambelli then announced that Mr. Perez-Olivo would be receiving the maximum sentence on the second-degree murder charge: 25 years to life. On the criminal possession of a weapon charge he received 15 years, to run concurrent with the murder conviction.

It was all over so fast in Courtroom 203. Not even ten minutes had passed since Judge Zambelli had called for order. Almost three weeks of testimony had come down to this. Had it been a movie, it would have been panned for its anticlimactic end.

Zambelli ordered the courtroom cleared for the rest of the day's business. Carlos, handcuffed once again, was led out of the courtroom. Looking over his left shoulder, he acknowledged his son Carlitos' presence. Carlitos responded with a sad smile. He looked to be on the verge of tears.

Janet DiFiore's PR spokesperson, Lucien Chalfen, announced that the district attorney would be making a statement regarding the verdict in the media room on the eighth floor of the county courthouse.

DA DiFiore read from a prepared statement:

> *"Mr. Perez-Olivo thought that he could—one final time—spin the events of that November night two years ago to his advantage, but the facts of the case told a different story.*

> *"The defendant meticulously planned and carried out the murder of his wife, weaving a web of deceit and concocting a story to cover up his actions. He believed that he would not be held accountable for the murder, which today's sentence of twenty-five years to life in state prison should serve to refute."*

CHAPTER THIRTY-EIGHT:

UNANIMOUS

JUROR NUMBER SIX made good on his civic obligation when, along with seventy-nine others, he appeared at the county courthouse on September 8, 2008, to be screened for jury duty. It didn't, however, prevent him from trying to be excused.

The 36-year-old Latino, who is an information technologist with a local charity, thought the estimated six weeks of trial would weigh too heavily on his employer. But since he was obviously a smart, technically savvy individual, he was too desirable to both the prosecution and the defense to be let go. Both sides wanted jurors just like him. As defense attorney Richard Portale said, they strived to seat jurors who could understand the technical testimony, such as ballistics and crime-scene forensics, that was sure to be presented.

Judge Zambelli apparently agreed and, after her standard speech on one's civic duty, refused his request for excusal. What was surprising about Juror Number Six—who wanted to remain anonymous—was the fact that he hadn't heard about the high-profile murder he was about to be asked to sit in and pass judgment on. "I'm not into that stuff," he later said. "I don't read those kinds of stories in the newspapers," adding wistfully, "Had I known about it, I probably would not have been picked."

There were no "Twelve Angry Men" on this panel. Number Six said his fellow jurors had gotten along "great." Many exchanged contact information and some friendships had been made. When ten of them got together along with

Number Six for the NBC *Dateline* interview, it was like a class reunion.

"We had worked together so well during deliberations that it was comforting seeing them all again," Six would say.

Juror Number Six said the defense had a "monumental task" in defending Carlos Perez-Olivo. The prosecution had made a strong circumstantial case against their client, and there was little the defense attorneys could do in refuting their accusations.

"It was pretty obvious to us [the jury] that he looked guilty. But we took all the time that we thought was necessary to give him his just due. We went back over each witness page by page, according to our notes, and we all took notes. We realized that he would be going away for a long time if found guilty, so we were careful not to make any mistakes."

Six said the totality of the testimony of all the witnesses was ultimately what "did him in," but one witness stood out above all others. That witness was Mark Gazzola.

According to the Dominican native, Gazzola had no stake in any of this. That he had seen the murder weapon in the defendant's possession a few months before the murder and had come forward to testify to that fact had impressed the panel.

Six remembered that it was Gazzola's testimony that was the first that pointed to Perez-Olivo as the trigger man in this case. Number Six said his knowledge of the gun, his unequivocal testimony and his apparent lack of any motive, other than his civic duty, for coming forward made him the star witness for the prosecution.

There were other witnesses who stood out. Six said Lieutenant Marc Simmons was very good and thorough. Six thought that Simmons had given Carlos the benefit of the doubt and treated him fairly. "Simmons wanted the truth and went about it in a professional way."

According to Six, not all of the prosecution witnesses were effective: "Out of all the expert witnesses for the prosecution, Brandi Benjamin raised some doubts. She was qualified, but compared to the other experts from the Westchester Lab, her testimony was kind of 'shaky.' It was because the [defense] lawyers rattled her some . . . It wasn't because she was lying or anything . . . It was just because she wasn't as experienced as her colleagues."

Six admitted he knew little about criminal justice, having never stepped foot in a courtroom before, so he could offer little in the way of criticism of the defense attorneys: "They were okay, and we could tell they were doing their best with what little they had. But they were always reaching, What if this . . . What if that . . . or the possibilities . . . The possibility of this . . . The possibility of that."

Six said that given the "concrete evidence" that the prosecution presented, the defense was forced to try to second-guess the witnesses or make the witnesses look less knowledgeable then they said they were. "I saw what they were trying to do, but it just didn't stick."

Juror Number Six had a lot of problems with Perez-Olivo's story of the altercation with the phantom gunman in the tight quarters of the Montero SUV. By far the most obvious problem with that story was that Peggy never woke from her slumber while her husband struggled with the armed intruder. Six said the alcohol imbibed in the city should not have incapacitated her to unconsciousness.

"And then all those gunshots happening! That didn't wake her? Then Mr. Perez-Olivo being dragged into the back of the car in very close quarters. That would have mangled his clothes, yet the cameras in the hospital show a very stylishly dressed defendant with his clothes in perfect order. It was like, Whoa! That kinda got us."

One of the jurors wanted to hear the 911 tape again to see how sincere Carlos Perez-Olivo was when he was making that phone call to the police.

"The problem with the nine-one-one tape," said Juror Number Six, "was that Perez-Olivo didn't give police any kind of direction of where he was and where he was going. He was very vague about his whereabouts. In the very beginning of the tape, when he said, 'Oh, hi, I think my wife has been murdered,' [he] sounded insincere."

The squabbling over the stippling around the victim's wound didn't impress this juror. He was convinced it was an execution type of wound, proven by the gunshot residue on the victim's headrest.

The defense's attempt to prove their contention of a struggle for the gun was a "reach," said the juror.

"The way the mannequin was placed inside of the car was like an impossible position to be in. It was unnatural."

Asked to explain why the jury had requested to examine the gun during the deliberating process, Juror Six explained that fellow jurors wanted to see the German markings on the gun and how it could have caused the slide bite on Perez-Olivo's left hand. Getting a closer look at the gun and how it worked, he said, seemed to confirm that slide bite was the probable cause of the wound.

Juror Six had heard the horror stories of how juries have not gotten along, or how they could not agree on anything. Things could not have been better with this jury. Juror Number Six related that when they sat down for the first time to deliberate, they agreed that all be given a couple of minutes where they would express their opinions about the case and how they were leaning regarding the defendant's guilt or innocence.

In the first go-around it was learned that all were leaning toward a conviction. They agreed, however, that they would comb through the whole case from the first witness to the last, and then make their decision.

It was Juror Number Six's idea to use the extensive notes that he and several other jurors had taken as a guide to rehash the case. That took all of the first day. They picked up where they'd left off the following Saturday morning.

Again, each juror was given the floor to express their views and what verdict they believed to be appropriate. All believed the defendant was guilty.

"We gave him [Perez-Olivo] his fair due," Juror Number Six said. "But to be sure, we went over it one more time."

There were no jurors who had doubts about the accused's guilt, but some were more convinced than others. Six said the strongest witnesses for the defense were Carlos' daughter Alysia and son Merced.

"They really hit home with us. Both got into our inner feelings and everything, and we saw how much they loved their father and believed him innocent. The picture they painted of him had some of us wondering that maybe he didn't do it."

Regarding the sensational testimony of Carlos' mistress, the jury was not prejudiced, said Juror Number Six. The only thing the prosecution got out of it was that the family was not perfect. "Just because he had an extramarital affair didn't mean he killed his wife," Juror Six said.

Speaking for himself, a Hispanic male, Juror Six said, "Men cheat, but that doesn't mean they will leave their wives, the main woman in their lives."

Juror Number Six believes they "got it right" when they convicted Carlos Perez-Olivo. The account of the gun and Perez-Olivo's version of what happened in that car were so full of holes that it sunk the defense's case.

"If they [the defense] had produced more witnesses who could say the defendant was a marked man, somebody who was out to get him because he was their criminal defense attorney, and the gun the Gazzolas saw that day was not the murder weapon, the verdict might have been different."

CHAPTER THIRTY-NINE:

BULLETS DON'T LIE

JUST FIVE MILES south of the crime scene on Route 9A/100 is a nondescript two-floor, red-brick building that houses the forensics and ballistics departments of the Westchester County Department of Safety. The building predates the 1979 merger of the county sheriff's department and the county parkway police; "Westchester County Parkway Police" is still etched in stone above the front door.

Anthony Tota has been plying his trade in the warren of security-protected rooms for nine years. Before that, he was with the New York City Police Department for thirty years doing the same thing—firearm ballistics. Tota is one of the most experienced ballistics experts in the country. Technologically, Tota says, the county is as sophisticated as the NYPD lab, just smaller.

Tota loves his work. A testament to that is the thirty years he put in with the NYPD, saying he could have taken his pension after twenty years, but he stayed another ten. When he retired, he tried a job in a pro shop at a golf range, but when the position opened up in Westchester, he jumped at the opportunity. Now, he says with a smile on his face, he is a lot closer to home in the northern end of the county.

The Ballistics Unit and the neighboring ID Unit, which handles latent fingerprints and crime-scene evidence, does most of the forensics work for the police departments within the boundaries of Westchester County. Tota describes his lab's work as firearm analysis and the analysis of evidence produced by firearms. His unit collects the evidence as well as analyzing it. Some of the county's bigger departments have their own crime-scene officers who will do the collection, but Tota and his fellow experts do all the lab work. The Ballistics Unit examines about 300–400 guns a year. Tota estimates that the average gun takes one to three hours of testing.

"We serve the forty-three jurisdictions in the county," Tota explains. "When they need us, they call us, or they bring the firearms here, we test-fire the gun and then we do the comparison work. We then put it all into the computer system and search the database for the pertinent information. We are always here. We rarely go out to a crime scene. In this particular case [Perez-Olivo] we were called out to examine the vehicle [the Montero SUV] at the impound lot."

Fellow Officer Artie Holzman of the Ballistics Unit received the .32-caliber Walther PPK semi-automatic pistol from the NCPD on November 23, 2006, Thanksgiving Day. The gun had been found the day before by the New York State Police Dive Team in nearby Echo Lake.

Holzman had removed it from the water in which it had been kept and flushed it with hot water to remove any contaminants. He'd dried it with pressurized air and then covered the piece with a fine layer of oil. That stopped the oxidation or the deterioration of the pistol. Holzman then examined the weapon to determine its "operability"—that is to say, if it was safe to fire. After finding the gun safe to handle, he delivered it next door to the ID Unit so it could be dusted for fingerprints.

The following Monday, the exact ammunition for the gun had to be purchased. For the common caliber guns, the unit has the appropriate caliber bullets on hand. That was not the case for the Walther, since it was a pre–World War II version and it fired the uncommon .32-caliber round.

The two men then took the weapon to the basement test room and fired a few rounds into the water tank and recovered the bullets for comparative analysis.

In the meantime the unit had received from the NCPD

the shell casings from the crime scene and the bullet from the medical examiner's office that they'd removed from the victim.

Several days later Holzman and Tota removed one bullet from the roof liner when they examined the vehicle that belonged to the Perez-Olivos. They had to remove the material first before the bullet could be pried out of the metal roof.

Being in the "business" for over forty years, Tota says he had seen this type of handgun many times. He calls it an "uncommon gun," but he makes a point of saying it is not a "rare gun." This particular Walther was a "sound" weapon. It had no visible cracks or damage, and was operable.

One floor below is the water tank, which measures 10'×4'×4'. Tota and Holzman fired several rounds into the test tank.

Next the test specimens were looked at under the microscope and compared to the bullets recovered from the crime scene and the victim, and determinations were made. Tota reported that the gun worked well, and the evidence received—three shell casings and two bullets—all came from the gun recovered from Echo Lake.

Tota explained that no two guns make the same marks on a projectile fired from them. Just like fingerprints or DNA, spent bullets are all unique. Tota gives a good example of this fact.

When he worked for the NYPD, the department was considering using the Glock as their standard-issue firearm. To be sure that the weapons could be checked for cut rifling—grooves in a fired bullet—his superiors asked Tota to perform some tests. Tota contacted Glock and requested that they supply him with three consecutively made gun barrels that were grooved with the same tool. Tota had a colleague fire nine shots, three from each barrel, and code each bullet so only he would know from what barrel they'd been fired. It took Tota twenty minutes to correctly identify which barrel each bullet had come from.

"It's that distinct," Tota said. "Sure, you'll get similarities, but if you examine the entire surface, you will find that the marks can't be reproduced. The bullets don't lie."

Anthony Tota and Artie Holzman produced test specimens not only for microscopic purposes, but also for distance and pattern tests. The pattern tests would tell them what that gun with that kind of ammunition would produce in the way of visible gunshot residue.

Ballistics experts can come to three conclusions: one, it's not the gun, two, it could be the gun and three, it is the gun. Both men concluded that the Walther from Echo Lake was the gun that had fired the bullets found at the crime scene.

Both Holzman and Tota conducted bullet trajectory examinations on the SUV while it was at the impound lot at the crime lab. They examined the bullet hole in the driver's-side rear fly window and the bullet hole in the roof liner.

The conclusion about the window hole was that the gun had been fired at the window at a 90-degreee angle, possibly when the door was open.

"The bullet struck the window straight on," Tota said. "There was no angle to it."

The defense ballistics expert, Dr. Harper, employed small cones that were inserted into the holes that the dowels were then fitted into. His examination concluded the bullet had come from below and exited the window at a steep angle.

"Not possible," said Tota. "Those cones he used were made of foam and had give to them. You could move them any way you wanted. The cones and dowels gave no reliable indication of an angled trajectory."

Holzman said that the window bullet hole was perfectly round with a crater on the exit side of the window of equal size all the way around, which indicates a straight-on shot. If it was an angled shot, the cratering would have been more pronounced on one side than on the other. It would be more of an oval hole than a round hole.

The only way the window bullet could have been the

one that struck Carlos was if he was kneeling up on the seat and directly in front of the window.

Holzman said the roof-liner material was never replaced over the hole by the defense expert when he made his calculations. The fabric was originally removed to access the bullet that was lodged in the metal roof and for a trace evidence search by forensics experts. The defense expert wound up making his determination on the impact hole without using the second point of reference, the material hole.

"To wind up with a very accurate trajectory, you have to have two points. We came up with the conclusion that it was fired upward at a fifteen-degree angle." Holzman added, "Since the defense expert never put the material back, he had only one point and he got inaccurate conclusions."

There were also gunpowder particles—burnt and unburnt—on the material, which gave them the distance from which the bullet was fired.

There was no speculation on the testers' part. When the roof liner was lined up with the roof hole, and with that ammunition and that gun, the dowels indicated how far the muzzle was from the impact area and what trajectory angle it was fired from. "You can't change the physical evidence to suit your theory of what happened," say the two experts. "It is what it is, and Carlos' story of what happened to that car cannot change it."

Tota says that "the less we know about what the police say, the victim says, and the suspect says, the better. I don't want to know what they said. We let the evidence speak [for itself]. If your story fits well with the evidence, then good for you. In this particular case, the story did not fit."

The two experts say the three shells and these two bullets came from the Walther, and the roof-liner hole had been shot from a 15-degree angle from fourteen inches away, the window hole from a straight 90-degree angle.

"That's it. There is no changing that," Tota says. "If you

can't come up with a story that fits within those parameters, then you are lying."

All of their work was peer-reviewed, then all the evidence was bagged and sealed, and the findings were reported to the NCPD and the Westchester County District Attorney's office.

On February 18, 2009, the National Academy of Sciences released a disturbing report on the 389 crime labs around the country.

The report said that ". . . with the single exception of DNA, no other crime-scene evidence is dependable enough to allow police officers to testify in court."

For two years, the panel of experts brought together by the National Academy of Sciences' National Research Council examined the country's forensic science system. Their report concluded that there was a need for an overhaul, which they said included mandatory accreditation, a national oversight committee and universal standards.

The report said that

> *forensic science is the application of scientific perspectives and methods to the investigative and legal process. However, it's become an umbrella term that encompasses disciplines of skill rather than real science. More alarming are a serious backlog of work and a lack of resources to address the needs. If forensic science loses credibility, the situation will only get worse.*

Harry T. Edwards is a federal appellate judge and co-chair of the committee that wrote the report. His panel concluded that there are too many scientists and other practitioners in the forensic science community who are strapped for funding.

The community is also fragmented, Edwards claimed:

> *Its practices are inconsistent, and its quality controls lacking. These shortcomings obviously pose a*

continuing and serious threat to the credibility of forensic science practice, i.e., a threat to people who might be sued or arrested for a crime in which scientific analysis is a component. It also hampers the prosecution of actual criminals.

The widely popular *CSI* TV series has made it hard for juries to shake images of the infallibility of science.

They've come to expect miracles and absolute certainty. But for the sake of justice and science, forensic experts need to be honest—in investigations and on the stand—about the limitations.

The report went on to state that the nation's crime labs are so seriously deficient that criminals are allowed to go free, the wrong people are sometimes convicted and only a "massive overhaul" can improve the results.

The panel members discovered that most crime labs are run by police or prosecutors, "which exert pressure to come up with specific conclusions."

The academy concluded:

The labs should be removed from the administrative control of law enforcement agencies or prosecutors.

Judge Edwards said that "science should serve the law. Law enforcement shouldn't drive the science."

In response to the findings of the Academy of Sciences, well-known defense attorney Barry Scheck warned that "we can't rely on judges, juries, prosecutors and defense lawyers in the cauldron of the courtroom to get to the bottom of what's wrong with certain forensic disciplines."

Danny Marrone, for one, was not surprised about the report's conclusions. Twenty-five years as a NYPD homicide detective and ten as a private investigator have taught him that when talking to crime-scene analysis experts, no two will agree on what the evidence shows.

"It is a lot of bullshit, and on their testimonies a lot of innocent people went to jail and a lot of bad guys got off. That this [crime analysis] is an exact science is a joke," Marrone said.

The report did not escape the attention of *The New York Times*. In an Op-Ed piece on February 21, 2009, the newspaper opened with the following:

> *It's not just that many forensic laboratories are poorly funded and staffed with "experts" who are poorly trained. The more fundamental problem, according to the study, is that there is little evidence of the accuracy and reliability of most forensic methods—especially those that rely on expert interpretation.*

The Westchester County lab "passed" on commenting on the report, leaving its public relations officer Kiernan O'Leary to relay the following:

> *Our crime lab, as well as the crime lab run by the County Department of Labs and Research, are both accredited by the American Society of Crime Laboratory Directors/Laboratory Accreditation Board. Both are also accredited by the New York State Division of Forensic Science.*

CHAPTER FORTY:

GOOD SCIENCE

> *"The most thoroughly validated technique is nuclear DNA analysis, which has a minuscule likelihood of error when done right. But other well-known methods that can supposedly identify a guilty person or link a weapon or other evidence to a particular crime have no rigorous scientific proof that they work consistently."*
>
> —*Op-Ed,* The New York Times, *February 21, 2009*

WITH A DOCTORATE in criminology in hand from the University of California, Berkeley, Peter R. De Forest first stepped foot in a crime lab back in 1960. At the time, crime forensics consisted of matching blood types and little else. Dr. De Forest has seen some momentous changes—many of which he was responsible for—in what is still a nascent science.

The now 66-year-old scientist has authored or co-authored several book chapters, a textbook, and numerous scientific articles. He has also served as a member of the editorial boards of journals including the *Journal of Forensic Sciences.* For over ten years, dating from the inception of the American Board of Criminalistics (ABC), Dr. De Forest served as the chairman of the ABC Examination Committee, which was responsible for designing and administering certification examinations in a range of forensic science specialties. He has lectured and given workshops for several professional societies and in other universities, and has served as visiting professor at the University of Strathclyde,

Glasgow, Scotland. During the fall 1997 semester he served as exchange professor with the National Crime Faculty at the Police Staff College, Bramshill, England, and also delivered the Founders Lecture for the California Association of Criminalists.

Retired as a professor of criminalistics from the world-renowned City University of New York's John Jay College of Criminal Justice, De Forest's résumé runs thirty-five pages long. He still does contract work for both the prosecution and defense in murder cases to opine as an expert witness. To date, he has testified in over two hundred trials. De Forest was also an official reviewer of the National Academy of Sciences' scathing report on the state of the nation's 389 crime labs.

He says the press articles on the report tend to focus on the negatives when there are a lot of good things in it.

The problem with the report, says De Forest, is that they had the wrong people writing it. They don't understand the nuances of the science. The choice of lawyers and scientists from other fields was wrong.

"It's like they brought in neurologists to write a report on nuclear chemistry," De Forest said. "It's not right. Criminal forensics is its own field, with its own unique problems. There are subtle things too, that you have to live with a long time to understand. The committee [National Academy of Sciences] was poorly put together. They did some good things, but a lot of it was counterproductive. The field needs some rethinking done, and that's what I'd like to do with my remaining time."

As to the opinion that the country's crime labs are under the thumb of police departments and district attorneys, he says this is "a big distortion."

He believes there have been cases where district attorneys have had too much sway with the labs, but it is the exception rather than the rule.

De Forest says coming to New York from California in 1969, he was appalled at the quality of the labs in the East. Their lack of a scientific perspective was pervasive. Today, he says, forensic scientists take great pride in their independence and dispassion.

"I have been a defense expert for many, many years," De Forest said recently. "By and large, the work that has been done in these labs is pretty good, and yes, occasionally there are some weaknesses that have been exploited by the defense. But these reports in the media are misdirected. There are problems in the field, no question about that, but they seemed to have missed the real problems."

De Forest says all forensic work is "pretty sophisticated stuff." On the surface, it would appear that it is pretty straightforward and not in need of scientific analysis. But, he adds: "It's when you get the real world stuff of partial fingerprints and such that you need scientists trained in the regimen to come to conclusions."

What worries Dr. De Forest about the academy's report is the real risk of resources being deflected away from things that need to be looked at. One of those things is the fact that a lot of labs don't have a scientific approach; the work is often left to retired cops with practical knowledge but not a lot of understanding of what they are doing.

"It's the whole thought process on how you solve a problem," De Forest explained. "A scientist would test the evidence several times, trying to prove the hypothesis wrong. He tries to destroy it. When it gets to the point that it can't be trashed, then you have something."

De Forest says the Westchester County lab is "pretty good," and staffed by many of his former students from John Jay College. When Fred Drummond headed the lab, he established a scientific environment there.

"When I came in there on a case I was working for the defense, they were very aboveboard on things, and we discussed the case openly. Since I did a lot of this work all over the country, I had a pretty good standard of comparison. The Westchester lab is one of the better ones."

De Forest, however, said that the lab should not be under the umbrella of the county police and should be separate as a stand-alone scientific workplace.

* * *

Dr. De Forest was called in late by the defense attorneys on
the Perez-Olivo case. For reasons not divulged, the defense
never called the professor to the stand. Bound by professional ethics, he would not disclose specifically what he'd
discovered in the course of his investigation. What he would
say was that the prosecution's forensic evidence didn't prove
anything, and could be interpreted a number of different
ways.

The veteran forensics expert did have a chance to examine the vehicle's headrest. De Forest says one of the things
that should have been pointed out by the defense was that
the execution-like fatal shot could have been the result of the
gun firing in the struggle that Carlos described.

The gunshot residue on the headrest does seem to
prove that the weapon was fired at a very close distance, but
that doesn't mean it could not have happened during the
struggle.

Peggy Perez-Olivo's fatal wound, in De Forest's opinion, showed no signs of stippling. De Forest has conducted
experiments that proved a head of hair can block the stippling effect from happening, even with large-caliber guns.
Peggy Perez-Olivo was killed with a small-caliber weapon.

"There's a huge misunderstanding when it comes to
stippling," says De Forest. "You have pathologists talking
about it that have never done the experiments. And then to
come to conclusions on it from photographs where the details are not good is bad science. From a photograph you
can't understand what each individual point is, whether it is
an actual hemorrhage or a little blood around a hair follicle.
Certainly you can't opine on it in front of a jury."

In regard to the defense's demonstration of Carlos' awk-
ward, contorted position in the back seat during the struggle
with his alleged assailant, De Forest says it could have happened.

"You have to remember when people try to do these stagings, it may not be possible to mimic the same position that was established through the actual body in one moment in time. Getting somebody or a mannequin in that same exact position is nearly impossible, because it could have happened in some kind of unsustainable orientation. Everything that happened in the SUV can be explained by the defense, as it can by the prosecution."

As to the trajectory of the bullet through the car window, De Forest says the angular differences would be very small when calculating the bullet's path. Using the cones to center the probe would thus have no real meaning, and would neither prove nor disprove the defense or the prosecution's contention.

"You can never get a precise trajectory angle anyway, so it's not a very significant thing to stress between having the cone in place or not," De Forest said.

That there was no blood on the back seat to indicate Carlos had been shot there, as he'd claimed, does not trouble Dr. De Forest. He was wearing two shirts and was shot by a small-caliber weapon—perhaps the shirts absorbed a lot of the blood. Also, this struggle happened in just seconds, and often it takes a while for a gunshot wound to bleed externally.

De Forest's opinions were just more proof of Private Investigator Danny Marrone's claim that, at least as far as the Perez-Olivo case is concerned, no two forensic guys can agree on one piece of evidence.

"It makes all the evidence in this case suspect, and certainly provides a juror with a reasonable doubt," the veteran homicide investigator said.

CHAPTER FORTY-ONE:

MEDIA STAR

JUST SIX WEEKS after the verdict, on November 11, 2008, Carlos gave an "exclusive interview" with the local CBS News TV program. Carlos, dressed in a bright orange jail jumpsuit and sitting at a table with his hands clasped, claimed with a plaintive face that the "real killer" was still running free.

He, however, waxed philosophic about his situation, saying, "You take all the indignities, and all the humiliation, and you live with it, because in your heart you know once you get to trial, you'll be redeemed."

Carlos said he was still angry at the guilty verdict, adding, "You know, it's a nightmare. I try not to think of it, because when I think of it, it's very hard. It's very hard to deal with. What happened with all the evidence presented to them that clearly showed not guilty?"

Switching subjects deftly, Carlos changed his tone to nostalgic, saying his wife was "a wonderful, wonderful mother and a great wife." He also said Peggy was "a savvy woman who would have sensed if I was plotting against her. She would have known if she was in any type of danger. She wasn't a simpleton."

Carlos did admit he had been involved in an extramarital affair with a woman young enough to be his daughter. His contrite tone clashed with the fact that it was not an aberration, but an affair that had lasted a decade.

Carlos and Peggy's second-oldest son Merced also appeared in the segment, where he expressed his support for his dad, saying, "I know in my heart there is no way my father could have done this."

The piece of evidence cited by the jury as the most incriminating was the handgun found in Echo Lake. In his TV interview, Carlos claimed the testimony linking him to the gun was false, adding, "There's absolutely no doubt that they know, and I know, what they said there was a lie." He did not elaborate for the camera.

Carlos said he spent a lot of his time in jail thinking about what he would say to the judge at sentencing. He also claimed he kept himself busy with the free legal work he did for the inmates who sought him out.

The TV interview culminated with Carlos saying that he worried about his children and how they were dealing with their mother's absence and their father in jail. Before the camera cut to the studio anchors, he added, "At least I can still set an example for them. No matter how much life can be cruel, and destroy you, you just keep fighting."

CHAPTER FORTY-TWO:

THE MURDER WEAPON

CARLOS SAYS HE knows what the Gazzolas saw, and it was nothing like what they testified to in court.

"First of all," Carlos related, "anybody [who] knows me, knows that I have never owned a gun, had a gun—I don't like guns. So the testimony of Mark Gazzola, saying I was in possession of one, is false."

Carlos reasoned that being a criminal defense attorney, he would have known better than to discuss an unregistered gun with a stranger.

According to Carlos, he had gone back to the house on Devoe Road on the day of the move because he had forgotten something, a very big something: he had left $18,000 in cash bundled up in aluminum foil and stashed in the attic between the ceiling joists and stuffed under the insulation. It had been the best hiding place he could think of.

Arriving back at the house, he immediately went up to the attic to retrieve his cash. The Gazzolas, Mark and father Gianfranco, were in one of the rooms on the second floor, cleaning. With the stash of money, Carlos had also hidden a pellet gun that belonged to his son Merced. The pellet gun was a concession to his son, who had pleaded with his dad for a firearm. The gun, he said, looked like the real deal.

Carlos tucked the bag of cash and the pellet gun under his left arm and carefully made his way down the steep folding attic staircase. The Gazzolas, alerted by the noise in the attic, came out to see who was in the recently vacated house.

According to Carlos, Mark Gazzola saw the pellet gun and remarked that he was into guns and was interested in what Carlos cradled under his arm. Because Carlos was in a rush to get out of the house, he had not zipped up the cash bag. He used the pistol to cover it so the Gazzolas wouldn't see the stacked bills. Carlos did not want to remove the gun to show it, so, mumbling an excuse that he had to be going, he hustled down the stairs and out to his waiting car. Carlos hated to be impolite, but he didn't know the two men and he did not want to advertise the fact that he was in possession of a bag of cash.

Carlos insisted in a one-on-one interview at the Valhalla that the pellet gun was the only "gun" in the house that Mark Gazzola could have seen. Carlos did concede that it looked a little like the murder weapon, but it most certainly was not a Walther PPK.

Carlos also thought the fact that Gazzola had waited until after Christmas to report the gun story to police was suspicious.

Ultimately Carlos and his defense team thought that the Perez-Olivo children's testimony had effectively negated the Gazzolas'. All three of them had said their father had never owned a gun or had one in the house, and that he hated guns.

That Gazzola insisted, after examining the murder weapon on the stand, that it was the same gun he'd seen five months earlier is incomprehensible. How, Carlos wondered, could he be so sure? "There just is no way that he could be sure it was the same gun."

According to Carlos, the discrepancies of both of the Gazzolas' testimonies should have negated the contention that the murder weapon had been in the hands of the accused. The father, Gianfranco, claimed it was in a box, and his son said it was in an envelope. Also, Gazzola said the gun that he'd seen at the Devoe Road house did not have the pinky grip on the bottom of the ammunition clip, yet the one presented in court as the murder weapon did have it. It was a statement that should have called Gazzola's testimony into question. When pressed on this discrepancy, Gazzola claimed it was just after Christmas when he'd given the initial description of the gun, and he was "nervous." The proper answer, Carlos contended, was "Well, maybe I said that then because I don't remember seeing the pinky thing, but it's the same gun, because it usually doesn't have it."

That Gazzola testified that the gun found at the bottom of Echo Lake was the same one he'd seen at the Devoe Road house troubled PI Danny Marrone as well.

For one thing, said Marrone, Gazzola was not a serious gun collector, and certainly not the expert he painted himself to be for the jury. Marrone knew that because he had pulled a copy of Gazzola's New York State pistol permit, a permit that was required to list all his handguns.

"They were all crap," said the PI of Gazzola's collection. "There wasn't one collectible in the bunch."

Furthermore, Marrone had owned a few Walther pistols over the years. Having read Gazzola's statement made before the grand jury, where he'd claimed that the Walther PPK was a rare firearm, Marrone thought, "What bullshit!" Marrone could go onto the Internet and within minutes find dozens of guns like the one in question up for sale. To prove his point, Marrone bought one for $700.

Marrone explained the difference between the "PP" and the "PPK." The PP was the German services handgun that was issued to detectives. The "PPK" (*Polizeipistole Kriminalmodell*, or Police Pistol Detective Model) was the civilian model, which had one less round in the magazine. Because it carried seven rounds instead of eight, the grip was shorter, and that is why "slide bites" were common with the PPK. What Walther did was put the PPK slide on the PP frame, which gave the PPK model the extra round and a longer grip, thereby reducing the chance of slide bite.

To Marrone, and defense attorneys McClure and Portale, that proved Gazzola to be no judge of what was a valuable and rare handgun, and thus, his description of the gun he'd allegedly seen at the house on Devoe Road was at best questionable.

The defense got further proof from the NCPD that the gun was misrepresented in Mark Gazzola's testimony. They found the important piece of information in the form of a handwritten three-page statement buried in a mountain of evidence turned over in the discovery phase by the DA's office. The statement was written by Earl Sheehan, a gunsmith from Tewksbury, Massachusetts.

Earl Sheehan is the owner of Earl's Repair Shop in Tewksbury, which is the exclusive factory repair station for Walther firearms in the United States. Sheehan, who claims to have been "around guns" since the age of 6, has owned and operated the shop for thirty-nine years. His experience makes him the foremost authority on Walther handguns in the country.

In his statement, Sheehan wrote that on Tuesday, April 10, 2007, at 11:25 AM, Detective Sergeant Marc Simmons and Detective Corrado of the New Castle Police Department walked into his northeastern Massachusetts shop and produced a Walther pistol in a sealed plastic bag. Cutting the bag open with a knife, Simmons, after identifying himself and his partner, asked Sheehan to examine the pistol.

Sheehan knew the small-caliber gun well. It consisted of a PP frame made in 1939, and a PPK slide. It could not have been military-issue, because it lacked the military acceptance markings. All parts on the frame, except the barrel and the internal de-cocking piece, are original to the frame. The grips were recognizable as World War II-era, since the "Walther" banners are larger on the post-war models.

Sheehan explained that to fit the PPK slide to the PP frame, a gunsmith would have to replace the spring and make adjustments to the barrel. The work could easily be done by a qualified gunsmith in an hour and a half, Sheehan estimated. The advantage of matching a PPK slide to a PP frame would be creating a "more concealable weapon."

But being more concealable would cause problems for the manufacturer later on. Since the slide contains the firing pin, breech face and extractor, changing it to a PPK slide would alter the ballistic fingerprint. Therefore, Sheehan stated, had the gun with the original slide been used in the commission of a crime, it would have been difficult to trace its lineage.

There were other possible reasons for mix–matching parts on the gun, Sheehan explained. During the war, because of the constant bombing of factories by the Allies, the Germans were forced to cannibalize guns for parts. "It was a common practice," Sheehan said, where you could get a working handgun out of the parts of three. After the war, many such hybrids found their way to the United States.

Sheehan would later say that the gun was a "scrap piece," and that there were "thousands of them around," making it virtually worthless to a collector. To enter Sheehan's report on the gun, which would have been a solid counter to Mark Gazzola's testimony, Sheehan would have had to testify.

Due to tardiness in getting some of the discovery evidence from the DA's office, the defense was unable to reach Sheehan in time. Danny Marrone, the defense's private investigator, tried to reach Sheehan several times over the course of a month. In his last attempt to reach him just prior to the start of the trial, he got a recorded message saying that Sheehan was "on vacation." Marrone suspected the Westchester DA's office was putting the potentially damaging witness "on ice," by putting him up at an unknown location or encouraging him to take a vacation during the trial, thereby making him unavailable to testify. Sheehan denied the allegation, and would not speak of any contract work he did for the NCPD or the Westchester County District Attorney's office, saying it was "proprietary information."

There was, however, another logical explanation for the mixed-parts gun. After a flurry of strict gun laws proposed by Congress after the assassinations of Martin Luther King, Jr., and Senator Robert Kennedy, the Gun Control Act of 1968 passed both houses and was signed into law by President Nixon. The Walther PPK failed to make the strict import requirements mandated by the law because of its light—hence concealable—weight. But if the frame from a PP replaced the PPK one, it made it heavy enough by one ounce to pass import restrictions.

Prior to the visit to the Massachusetts gunsmith, Simmons had the Bureau of Alcohol, Tobacco and Firearms run a trace on the murder weapon. In December of 2006 the firearms technology advisor reported that the gun was sold by the German manufacturer to the importer Interarms of Alexandria, Virginia, in 1966. Interarms subsequently sold the gun to Richard Sales Company of Shaker Heights, Ohio. However, the firearms dealer in Ohio, which is now out of business, had no records for the time frame during which this firearm was sold by them. The advisor said that, since record-keeping requirements were not mandated by federal law at that time, the gun in question could not be traced further. It, in effect, dropped out of sight in 1968 until it was retrieved from the bottom of Echo Lake on November 22, 2006.

Originally designed Walther PPs and PPKs had a small "tang" just above the grips that prevented the shooter from grabbing the gun incorrectly. In firing the weapon, the slide would be blown back with the ignition of gases and in the process extract the empty shell casing, ejecting it, then reloading another bullet in the chamber on its return trip along the top of the frame. If the hand extended over the tang, the slide would "bite" the hand, usually producing a painful abrasion on the webbing between thumb and forefinger. Later designs extended the tang for obvious reasons.

The murder weapon was an older version that Marrone said had a tendency to cause such a wound, a wound that Carlos appeared to have on his left hand. But Carlos said he'd gotten stung there when the gun went off while he was struggling with the intruder. It was definitely a possibility, especially since Perez-Olivo was right-handed, reasoned Marrone. Besides, he found Carlos to be a "straight-talking good guy who seemed to have been already found guilty by the media." Examples of this were legion, and Marrone cited two that irked him: media types always described the defendant as "the disbarred lawyer" and the only video they ran of him on the news programs was the one of him in the altercation during which Carlos took a swing at a reporter.

* * *

That the jury found Gazzola believable was in itself incomprehensible to Carlos.

It was also absurd, Carlos said, that a gun would be left out in the open by the movers. Somebody, he insisted, would have picked it up before the Gazzolas discovered it in the upstairs bedroom closet.

Carlos, as he had said in the disbarment hearings, claimed that a lie-detector examination of both he and Gazzola would have shown who was lying about the gun. All it would have taken was both parties' consent to be questioned while hooked up to the machine. Carlos was willing, but the district attorney's office was not.

CHAPTER FORTY-THREE:

PRISON

MISSION STATEMENT

Enhance public safety by providing appropriate treatment services, in safe and secure facilities, that address the needs of all inmates so they can return to their communities better prepared to lead successful and crime-free lives.

> —A sign posted at the front gate of the
> Wende Correctional Facility, Alden, NY.

Downstate Correctional Facility is one of just a very few reception and classification processing centers operated by the NYS Department of Correctional Services. During intake, an extensive review of an inmate's pre-sentence report and other documented findings is conducted. This review, at times, alerts staff of the potential security concerns, including but not limited to a person's enemy list, a person's former employment, a person's notoriety, etc. If the Department believes any of these factors is a concern, an inmate may be placed into protective custody.

So wrote Linda M. Foglia, Assistant Public Information Officer, New York State Department of Correctional Services, Office of Public Information.

Downstate was where Carlos found himself after being taken from Westchester County custody and transferred into New York State's prison system. The prison, as the name suggests, is in the state's lower tier, about 50 miles north of New York City and less than thirty minutes' drive from Chappaqua. Directly across I-84 is the medium-security Fishkill Correctional Facility, which houses 1,475 general confinement inmates. It's also the site of the 100-bed disciplinary housing unit for inmates serving 90 days or more disciplinary confinement. This property also operates the area's Regional Medical Unit. The only real connection between it and Downstate is the fact that they're both operated by the DOC. They don't share staff, inmates or even equipment.

At Downstate there are presently 1,230 prisoners, but Carlos has little or no contact with the general population. He sits in another section of the facility with just eighteen other inmates, the Protective Custody (PC) unit.

Usually an inmate's stay is a brief one at Downstate, as explained in Ms. Foglia's missive. Downstate, being that it is a "processing center," is step one in the systematic absorption of convicted criminals into the state's enormous penal population. But since the facility has one of the largest and latest PC wings, Carlos expects to be there until the bureaucratic DOC decides what maximum-security prison is best suited for him.

The PC wing can house thirty-six inmates, mostly pedophiles, convicted cops and high-profile prisoners who might as well have targets on their backs. The state doesn't like their charges getting themselves killed. It reflects badly on their record, hence the segregation of the vulnerable.

According to the DOC, bed space availability, program needs (counseling, education), mental health, physical health, instant offense, sentence (always a maximum if a sentence is 6 or more years before parole eligibility), risk assessment, enemies, notoriety, etc. have to be considered when determining if an inmate should get protective custody.

Downstate keeps the inmates generally from two to six weeks before they are moved to a facility where they will serve out their sentences.

For Carlos, the unending boredom that he endures is his punishment. As an inmate under protective custody, he never leaves the wing. Prisoners housed there eat, sleep, exercise and socialize with other inmates all within the secured wing. Carlos, however, does little socializing. He finds that the other inmates are for the most part uneducated and uninteresting. They spend most of their time, he says, with their eyes glued to the TV set, which usually is tuned to game shows or soap operas. Consequently Carlos whiles away the day reading books in his 9×4–foot cell. He averages a book a day, and is continually on the prowl for new material.

Carlos worries about his family, Alysia particularly so. Still a child, in his view, at 20 years, she is attending school in Canada. She misses her family terribly. Her Aunt Laura says she received a call from Alysia recently. The girl wanted her mother's sister to tell a story about her mom because "she was really missing her a lot today."

Her aunt continues, "She is still very vulnerable. Alysia is right on the edge and can go either way. Merced is too, but he is also very angry and hurt. They are alone and don't have a lot of support."

Carlos had noticed that there was blood in his urine. Since he had always been an athlete who took pride in taking care of himself, the bleeding concerned him. After a preliminary examination by prison doctors, it was decided that a biopsy of his prostate had to be done. The results were not good. The urologist concluded that he had cancer. His doctor was a "very compassionate man," says Carlos, and with obvious difficulty told him the bad news. Carlos was almost flippant about the grim tidings.

"After losing my wife and now my children," Carlos explained, "prostate cancer was the least of my concerns."

On a Tuesday, he was returned to prison, where he was told that he was going to be transferred to another correctional facility, presumably Clinton in northern New York near the Canadian border. Clinton had a state-of-the-art hospital ward where Carlos could be treated.

Carlos was kept in isolation for the next two days: no visitors, no phone calls.

On February 20, 2009, with just the clothes on his back, he boarded a DOC bus and was shackled into his seat. The bus made two stops at other facilities along the way to pick up and drop off prisoners. In Elmira, New York, he and the remaining three prisoners were transferred to a van. After nine hours, Carlos arrived at the Wende Correctional Facility, a maximum-security prison that sits amidst the rolling farmlands of western New York, just twenty miles east of the city of Buffalo.

Wende Correctional Facility is located in the Town of Alden in Erie County. Like most prisons, it has an interesting history.

Gangster Jimmy Burke, mastermind of the 1978 $6 million Lufthansa heist, was imprisoned in this facility until his death in 1996. At the time, the heist was the largest cash robbery in American history. Burke was made famous by Robert De Niro's portrayal of him in the box-office smash hit *Goodfellas*.

Jack Henry Abbott was another notorious inmate at Wende. Abbott was a convicted killer and best-selling author of *In the Belly of the Beast*, a prison journal. He had been paroled in 1981 after the efforts of acclaimed novelist Norman Mailer, who believed Abbott to be a brilliant writer. After just six weeks back on the street, Abbott knifed to death a New York City waiter, Richard Aden, 22, over a disputed check. In January 1982 Abbott was convicted of first-degree manslaughter and sentenced to 15 years to life at Wende.

The prison-hardened author was found hanging from a makeshift noose constructed from bed sheets and shoelaces in his prison cell on February 10, 2002. The prison authorities ruled it a suicide. The 58-year-old inmate left a note, though its contents were never disclosed.

An attorney who had been helping Abbott with a lawsuit against the state for a serious beating he'd suffered at Attica Correctional Facility in 2000 publicly expressed doubt that Abbott had committed suicide. He said Abbott had spoken to him of fears for his safety in the weeks leading up to his death.

Norman Mailer had this to say about Abbott's violent life, as quoted in *The New York Times*:

> *"His life was tragic from beginning to end," Mr. Mailer said yesterday in a prepared statement. "I never knew a man who had a worse life. What made it doubly awful is that he brought a deadly tragedy down on one young man full of promise and left a bomb crater of lost possibilities for many, including most especially himself."*

Due to a growing inmate population, the state began an expansion of maximum-security prisons in the early 1980s. The Department of Corrections purchased the Erie County Penitentiary in 1983 from Erie County for $48 million.

Wende houses three distinct inmate populations: general confinement, maximum-security inmates; a reception center for western New York inmates; and Special Needs Unit (SNU) inmates, a population comprised of individuals who have various developmental and other learning disabilities.

The prison is staffed with just over 800 employees, 527 of whom are security staff.

Disrobing in front of the guards, Carlos took a cold shower, where he was told to wash his hair with an antiseptic shampoo. After toweling off, he was issued his new clothing and then his head was shaved, as was his beard. Issued his ID, he was then marched off to his block. Carlos says the whole process was "curt and abrasive," as it was intended to be. He understood why. New inmates have to prove themselves to be trustworthy and not discipline problems. Then, and only then, are they treated with respect.

Carlos had objected initially to his protected custody status. He felt he got along well with his fellow inmates and he didn't want to be labeled a "PC" inmate due to the fact that most inmates with that designation were at the bottom of the prison hierarchy: pedophiles, child killers and rapists. But it was explained to his satisfaction that he would be at risk in the general population because of his notoriety. Killing or beating a famous inmate was a way for violent prisoners with nothing to lose to make a name for themselves in a facility. There were also the threats from disgruntled former clients, many of them in jail, whom the prison authorities had to worry about.

The PC unit at Wende is a very small unit (DOC does not release specifics about the unit for security purposes) and the cells are tiny, about half the size of his at Downstate. He is locked down for twenty-two hours a day. The unit does have a larger exercise yard than Downstate; consequently Carlos is able to run laps and get some sun.

Things are less strict at Wende than at Downstate. In Carlos' unit, prisoners are continually yelling back and forth all day long. You can stay up as long as you want and sleep all day if you prefer. Downstate was more regimented because the DOC, according to Carlos, "wants to break you in" early on in your sentence. The guards there were very strict, since it is a transitional facility where they don't have enough time to get to know an inmate and determine if he is a problem prisoner. At Wende, prisoners and guards settle in for the long haul, where they can get the measure of each other and act accordingly. Carlos says most of his guards are civil, some even sympathetic.

Carlos was sent to Wende because the medical facilities that can treat his cancer are the best the system has to offer. Given his options on treatment (surgery, chemotherapy, radiation), he opted for radiation. For the next five months,

Carlos would be radiated Monday through Friday at a Buffalo area hospital. Carlos says his treatment could not be
better. If only his legal problems were given as much attention, he says.

In the exercise yard there are two pay phones that inmates
can use, first come, first served. From an approved list, Carlos can make collect telephone calls. On every other night
after 7 PM he can make calls from an inside phone. His calls
generally run twenty minutes. He spends the most time con-
versing with his son Merced, who seems to relish conversations with his father. Carlos says he has to be careful with
daughter Alysia. She is still young and has a fragile psyche,
due to the circumstances of her life. Carlitos has proven to be
more difficult to talk to because of his career and marriage.
The written word has been their means of communication.

"Carlitos has his own life," Carlos explained, "and he
doesn't need me as much as Merced and Alysia do. It's sad
to say, but in some ways it's much easier for me to deal with
being incarcerated talking to nobody. I'm torn, since there is
very little I can do for them besides being a familiar comforting voice on the phone. The calls are stressful and very
emotionally draining, but I do it because it's important for
them and me. Jailed here, if I didn't have my kids, it would
be like being dead."

Carlos wants to see his daughter, but he is concerned
how she would react to the prison: its tangible grimness, the
walls, the bars and the razor-wire fences that surround it. It
may be too much for the impressionable young girl. Yet he
feels that because he was so protective of his daughter and
his wife, he says, Alysia has gotten some good out of the
tragic situation: she has learned to fend for herself. A sad
half-smile graces his face as the irony of it hits home.

Progress on the appeals process has been slow. Defense Attorney Chris McClure had told Carlos that all the paperwork

on the appeal would be finished by the end of December 2008. Carlos gave his lawyer until the end of January before he would agitate for action. On a legal visit from family attorney and friend Robert Buckley on March 4, 2009, Carlos was told that McClure hadn't started the appeal process.

"I went nuts!" Carlos said. "I've been sitting in prison for three months twiddling my thumbs. The money was there to pay for it, and I want those guys. They know the case, and they worked hard on it leading up to and during the trial."

But the appeal would be handled differently. That much he knew.

Carlos believes in retrospect that his defense team played it too conservatively. If granted a new trial, he is determined to play a more active role in his defense and push for a more aggressive tack in bringing witnesses forward to testify.

Carlos finds it particularly galling that he is in prison for killing his wife, the woman, he says, who was the love of his life. If he had been convicted of killing anybody else, however unjustly, he feels he could deal with it—but not for the murder of Peggy.

"If you talked to anybody who knew us, they would tell you I couldn't hurt her. She, along with my children, was the most important person in my life. The irony of it—the cruelty of it—drives me crazy. How can this have happened to me?"

Carlos is not optimistic about what lies in store for him.

"Logic tells me that there are good grounds for [acquittal on appeal], but somehow, because of the trial verdict, people will think I must be guilty because the jury said I was. I don't know what will happen. Half of me doesn't care anymore. Bottom line is that all this is my fault. It was somebody who was after me and if she hadn't been there, she would still be alive. There was a struggle, and I lost, and my wife paid for it."

What keeps the convicted murderer going is the goal of

keeping his children from having to have to visit him in prison for the rest of his life.

"I want to be out there for them and not locked up in a tiny cell waiting to die. They deserve better. Peggy was my motivation. She would have never let me quit and feel sorry for myself. I have to remember that."